READY TO

How to turn your (very) rough draft into a book

Dr Jennifer Jones

Printed in the United Kingdom First Printing, 2022

ISBN: 978-1-8380011-2-4 (Paperback) ISBN: 978-1-8380011-3-1
(eBook)

Maggie Cat Books St Columb
Cornwall TR9 6HW

jennifer@ewc.coach

For Maggie

Contents

SECTION 1: THINGS TO CONSIDER BEFORE YOU START

Chapter 1

WHO IS THIS BOOK NOT FOR?

T O HELP YOU MAKE the best use of your time, before I go further I want to establish who this book is not for.

This book isn't for novelists, short story writers, playwrights, screenplay authors, or poets. I only write nonfiction, so I only coach/write books about nonfiction.

Nor is this book for nonfiction writers who want to publish traditionally. When nonfiction writers seek to publish traditionally they first need to find an agent. Most agents don't want to read full manuscripts of nonfiction works (this advice does **not** apply to works of fiction). Instead, they want a detailed outline and a few sample chapters, amongst other things.

For nonfiction writers seeking traditional publishing contracts, there's no point in writing a full draft before you get an agent. Your agent will suggest changes to your outline/sample chapters and when you sign with a publisher, they'll require further changes. Writing a full draft before you get to that stage creates more work for you.

So while traditionally published nonfiction writers may find my advice on writing useful, this isn't the book you need to read while you're searching for an agent.

Chapter 2

WHO IS THIS BOOK FOR?

N OW THAT WE KNOW who this book isn't for, who is it for? It's for coaches, consultants, healers, and other people who help people who want to finish and self-publish their expert book.

An expert book is one that tells your current and potential clients what you do and why you do it that way. For your current clients, your book will serve as an excellent set of notes to help them remember what they've learned while working with you. For your potential clients, it will help them make an informed decision about working with you.

Why would they work with you if your book tells them everything? Because your book, excellent though it will be, isn't you. Your book can't help them understand how to apply your approach to solving their problem to their specific circumstances.

Authors of these kinds of books are better served by self-publishing than by going the traditional route. If you're thinking that it would have to be better to be published by one of the major publishing houses than to self-publish, keep reading.

The purpose of an expert book is to help your current and future clients. The purpose of a publishing house is to publish books that will make money for the publishing house.

In case the disconnect between those purposes isn't clear, I'll explain further. When you self-publish, you have the ability to publish exactly the book your clients/readers need to read from you. Your purpose in publishing is not to make money from book sales, but rather to use the book and the credibility it gives you to increase your visibility and your sales.

Meanwhile, a publisher is only concerned with their own sales. They're not concerned with giving your current and potential clients the book they need – they need to publish books that traditional booksellers believe they can sell.

In some rare cases, the book your clients need to read will be the book the publishers want to publish, but too often this is not the case. What happens when it's not? The author has to change the book to suit the publisher's needs, or they risk losing the contract (and face having to return any advance they were given).

There's also the question of timing. When you self-publish, you control (for the most part) how long it takes. Once you have the support you need in place (see chapter 7, 'Get support in place', for more on that), you control how long it takes. It's possible to get a well-written, fully edited book out in just a few months.

When you go the traditional route, your book is made to fit into other people's schedules. It can take 12 to 18 months to find an agent and then take your agent 6 to 12 months to find you a publisher (most publishers will not look at queries that come directly from authors). Once you have a contract with a publisher, you have to write the book (to their specification) and then wait for it to go through their production process. If everything goes smoothly, you're looking at 2 ½ to 3 years between your first query letter to a potential agent and publication day.

Remember, when you get to publication day as a traditionally published author, you'll have a book that you can be proud of, but it's unlikely to be exactly the book your clients/readers need from you. Also, since a self-published book can go from vague idea to a real book in your readers' hands inside of 6 months, readers of your traditionally published book will have to wait an extra 2+ years!

Chapter 3

How long will it take?

T O HELP YOU CALCULATE how long it will take you to get your book into your reader's hands if you start work on it today, see the chart on page 16. Alternatively, you can download a copy here: https://ewc.coach/ready-to-publish-resources/

To help you fill in that chart, read on to find out how long each of the steps outlined in 'Section 2: Step-by-step instructions to finding your book' is likely to take.

1. **Make your book work for you and your business.** Don't skimp on this – set aside 2 to 3 hours to plan how to use your book to increase your visibility right now and think about where it fits in your business. Is your book the entry level product that will make it easier for future clients to buy your higher ticket services? Or is it your ticket to speaking on bigger stages? Or both? After the initial 2 to 3 hours, plan to come back to this question at least once a month to make sure your book is working for you (even before you've published it). **Time: 2 to 3 hours initially; then 20 to 30 minutes a month.**

2. **Manage your time.** Use the steps in this section to help you break the task of publishing your book down into small, achievable steps. Then schedule them in your diary so you have time to complete each one. **Time: 2 to 3 hours.**

3. **Get support in place.** If you've never published a book before and you're doing this without the aid of a coach, you'll need several hours to research which editors, book formatters/consultants, and cover designers to approach. You'll then need a couple of hours for correspondence as you get each piece of support in place. Finding beta readers is typically less time consuming, assuming you know where your ideal reader hangs out (think which social media platforms they're on, which Facebook groups they're in, and which networking events they attend), then it's a matter of reaching out to people who would be suitable beta readers. If you already know these people, your active time in securing beta readers will be as little as an hour, but if you don't know them, it could take considerably longer. If you're working with a coach, all of these processes can be sped up considerably (and it may be a service your coach offers – it's one I offer my clients). **Time: 2 to 16 hours.**

4. **Your ideal reader.** You'll need at least an hour or two for this step. If you've written a book before and are already familiar with a version of your ideal reader, it will be quicker. If this is your first

book, it will take a little longer. **Time: 1 to 2 hours.**

5. **What does your reader need?** This is when you decide which of your reader's problems your book is going to solve. **Time: 1 hour.**

6. **Focus and outline your book.** This one has two steps: (1) statement of argument: though this involves writing only one sentence, it is the most important sentence in your entire book (it forms the foundation for your outline), so don't rush it. Give yourself at least an hour. (2) Rough outline: This stage involves asking all the questions you'll need to answer about your statement of argument to convince your reader that you're right. Set aside 1 to 2 hours. **Time: 2 to 3 hours**

7. **Check your draft against your rough outline.** How long this takes will vary according to how long your draft is and how quickly you read. Note that this is not a detailed read, you're just checking the sense of what you've written, you are *not* editing your work. Most readers will need 4 hours to go through a 100-page draft at this level (if you read slowly, or just don't like to read on screen, use the text to speech function in Word or Google Docs). **Time: 4+ hours.**

8. **Fill any gaps identified in the previous step.** How long this will take depends on how many

gaps you found, so I won't attempt to estimate it here. **Time: variable.**

9. **First revision.** How long this takes depends on how long your manuscript is and what condition it's in (i.e., are you working with unedited transcripts or material you wrote for your book?). **Time: approximately 6 to 8 hours.**

10. **Polish.** Don't get bogged down here – your book is still going to your editor later. I'll break this estimate down by subsection: (1) chapter titles and subheadings, give yourself 30 to 45 minutes; (2) permissions and referencing, depending on the type of book you're writing, this might take an hour, or several days. See pages 108-13 for help estimating how long it will take you. Whatever you do, don't skip this – doing so could have serious legal implications. (3) Sentence level revisions – for a 100 page manuscript, give yourself at least 6 hours. **Time: variable – from about 8 hours to several days.**

11. **Beta readers** – this doesn't require much of your time, but you'll need to allow 4 weeks in your timeline for your draft to be with your beta readers. Then you'll need to set aside about 5 hours to consider which of their suggestions you agree with and to apply them. **Time: 4 weeks inactive time + 5 hours active time.**

12. **Editor** – again, this doesn't require much of your time, but you'll need to allow at least 4

weeks in your timeline for your draft to be with your editor. Then you'll need to set aside about 8 hours to consider which of their suggestions you agree with and to apply them. **Time: 4 weeks inactive time + 8 hours active time.**

13. **Publish** – if you're sending your polished draft to a book formatter or publishing consultant, refer to their timelines to gauge when your book will be out. If you're doing it yourself, you'll want to set aside at least 20 hours (if it's your first book, you may need considerably more time than that). **Time: variable.**

How Long Will It Take?

1. Make your book work for you and your business:

   Initial time required:

   Ongoing commitment:

2. Manage your time:

3. Get support in place:

4. Your ideal reader:

5. What does your reader need?

6. Focus and outline:

7. Check your draft against your outline:

8. Fill gaps:

9. First revision:

10. Polish:

11. Beta readers:
    Inactive:

    Active:

12. Editor:
    Inactive:

    Active:

13. Publish:

Chapter 4

HOW WILL YOU FIND THE TIME?

N OW THAT YOU HAVE a rough idea of how long it will take you to finish your book, you need to have a think about how you work best.

Are you someone who prefers the little and often approach? Or would you rather just get stuck into the big project and largely ignore everything else until it's done?

I tend to favour the little and often approach. It is kinder on our schedules and allows us to make a bit of progress most days. All of those little bits of progress really add up quickly.

If that approach sounds like a slow kind of torture for you, you'll need to clear your schedule (as much as possible) for a couple of weeks to get your book to the stage that it's ready to go to your beta readers and then clear it again for a day between getting their feedback and sending it to your editor. And again when you get it back from your editor. To make this approach a little kinder on your schedule, you can outsource some of the steps, but that assumes you have the financial resources to do so. For example, if you have an assistant, they can research editors, cover designers, and book formatters – you could even pay for your assistant to complete my self-publishing course, Format and Publish Your Book,[1] so they could format and publish your book for you.

There is no right way to approach writing your book, but you will be a happier author if you choose the approach that best suits your life and your temperament. For help deciding which approach is best for you, see chapter 6, 'Manage your time'.

---

1. You can learn more about the course here:
   https://ewc.coach/format-and-publish-your-book/

SECTION 2: STEP-BY-STEP INSTRUCTIONS FOR FINDING YOUR BOOK

Chapter 5

MAKE YOUR BOOK WORK FOR YOU AND YOUR BUSINESS

T HIS MAY SEEM LIKE a weird place to start – how can you make a book work for you when that book doesn't even exist? Stay with me here.

You need to start here to help with your motivation and to start building your audience. If you launch your book to a cold audience you're not going to see any sales for a while.

For you

As you work on your book, you need to stay aware of what it is doing and can do for you personally. If you've ever struggled with imposter syndrome or a fear of visibility, writing your book will help you put those fears to rest.

I wrote my first book, *There's a Book in Every Expert (that's you!)*, before I started coaching people to write their books (no sensible person would hire a book coach who hadn't written a book!). Before I became a coach,

I was an academic, including working as a lecturer in English in US and UK universities from 2001 to 2016. So by the time I started coaching writers, I'd already taught hundreds of students how to be happier, more effective writers. Nevertheless, I was a bundle of nerves before my first coaching session, but I was able to stop the nerves by reminding myself that I'd literally written the book on what I was coaching.

Having published a book has also helped immensely with my stage fright – despite having been painfully shy at school and at uni, I'm now perfectly happy to talk to online or live audiences of any size. A large part of that is owing to my increased confidence after writing my book. When I'm hired to talk about writing, I don't have to wonder if I have enough to say to fill a whole hour – I've filled whole books (as of autumn 2022, I've filled 3 of them).

Take an hour or so to write about (or list) the various ways finishing your book will help you personally. Doing this will make it easier for you to stay motivated and to remember why you're putting so much effort into finishing your book. These questions might help you get started:

- Will it alleviate stress you routinely feel in your personal or professional life? How would life be different if you weren't wasting time and energy on that stress?

- How has having an unfinished book sitting on your hard drive affected you? Has it made you doubt your ability to follow through on important projects? Has it made you frustrated that you started something without having a clear plan for finishing it? How will finally finishing that thing feel? How much of an energy boost will you get from your sense of accomplishment?

For your business

You'll find more detail on using your book for your business in chapter 18, 'What now?', so I'll only briefly touch on those points here.

Your book is the ultimate marketing tool. Once it's done, you'll never again have to wonder what to post – you'll have 100+ pages of material that's always relevant to your business and your audience. This treasure trove of content will bring a new level of continuity to your marketing efforts that will make it easier than ever before for your potential clients to understand what you do and how you can help them. You can start developing that continuity of messaging by using excerpts from your draft in your social media posts! Make sure you mention that they come from your draft so you can get people to start thinking of you as an author.

Your book will establish your credibility with lots of people; here I'll focus on what it does for your speaking career (for more on credibility, see pages 181-3). If you're looking to increase your visibility by increasing the number of speaking engagements you do, adding 'author of {insert your title here}' to your speaker bio will cause your *yes*-rate to skyrocket. People looking for speakers (from podcast guests to keynote speakers at large conferences) want to know that you have a clearly thought out message. Having a book shows them that you do. You can start building that credibility before you hit publish by talking about your work on your book regularly – start now!

Finally, your book increases your reach. It allows those who can't or won't work with you to learn from you. That means you get to help more people than you could possibly coach. It also increases the number of people who are aware of what you can do – that leads to word of mouth referrals, which leads to more clients – all from someone who read your book but couldn't or wouldn't hire you for themselves.

Chapter 6

MANAGE YOUR TIME

N OW THAT YOU UNDERSTAND what your book will do for you and your business, we need to look at when and how you're going to manage your work on your book! To manage your writing time well and finish your book as quickly and efficiently as possible, you need to be clear on two things:

1. How you work best

2. Your publication timeline/deadlines

How you work best

When people ask me how I structure my writing time, they're often looking for a structure they can adopt for themselves – in the same way people try to adopt the morning routines of the highly successful.

Adopting someone else's routine rarely produces the same, or even comparable results because there are too many variables at play. My routine works for me because it works with my unique personality, psychological make up, and circumstances.

When I coach writers, I don't give them a set of prescriptive rules or routines to follow. Instead, we look at what has and hasn't worked well for them in the past (never skip this step). We then use that to develop a system or routine that will work for their current project.

How can you do this? Spend some time (no more than half an hour) thinking about these questions – if it helps, you can download them as a worksheet here: https://ewc.coach/ready-to-publish-resources/

1. Think of a large project (it needn't involve writing) that you completed successfully and (relatively) easily. How did you approach it? Was it your sole focus from the moment you started until you completed it? Or did you fit work time for the project in around other tasks, responsibilities, or interests? In other words, did you deliver the successful project using (a) an intensive, binge-working approach or (b) a little-and-often, snack-working approach? Neither approach is better than the other. Both can work, but they do not work equally well for all people.

2. How did you feel about the project while you were working on it? Since you've finished it?

3. How did you feel about the approach you took to at the time? Now?

4. Now think of a project you struggled with but completed. Did you use (a) an

intensive, binge-working approach or (b) a little-and-often, snack-working approach?

5. How did you feel about the project while you were working on it? Since you've finished it? How did you feel about the approach you took at the time? Now?

6. Did you use the same approach for the two projects? If not, were you happier/more successful with the project that used the approach you found more comfortable? If so, why was one project more of a struggle than the other? Was something different about your personal life or circumstances? Can you think of a time you've used the opposite approach? If not, you have a choice to make: (1) stick with what you know (it has been successful in the past) or (2) try the other approach for your book. Whatever you choose – if it's not working, change it. Your book is your project, and you get to decide how to do it.

Keep your notes on these questions to hand while you choose the approach that best suits your temperament and circumstances today.

What would finishing your book using the intensive, binge-working model look like?

The answer to that question largely depends on how much of your draft is done and what shape it's in – is it transcriptions from your course or more reader-friendly material that you've written or worked on in the past?

If your first draft is mostly done, you may need as little as 24 to 40 (working) hours to polish your draft enough to send it to your beta readers. Remember, for them, your draft needs to be intelligible, not as close to error-free as possible – getting it to that stage is your editor's job.

If you still have some drafting to do – unwritten chapters or significant holes to fill (see chapter 10, 'Check your draft against your book outline' for help with this), or you're starting with unedited transcripts – you may need 24 to 40 hours for drafting and a further 24 to 40 hours for revisions.

If spending 24 to 80 hours submersed in a project over the course of a week or two excites you, this is the approach for you.

If it sounds tolerable and suits your deadlines, it's for you, too.

If it makes you feel a bit ill, if at all possible, choose the other option.

What would using the little-and-often approach look like? You'd spread those same 24 to 80 working hours over several weeks.

How many weeks depends on how many days per week you want to work and how many hours you want to spend on your book on those days.

If you look at spreading 80 hours over 16 weeks (1-hour/day, 5 days/week) and cringe because you don't want your book to take that long, you're going to have to make some compromises like working on the book for 2 hours a day over 8 weeks.

Your deadlines

You need to understand how you can and want to work on your book *before* you book any of the help you need like cover designers, editors, beta readers, or book formatters (see chapter 7, 'Get support in place'). Once you've booked this support (and often have paid non-refundable deposits for their services), it's difficult (and potentially expensive) to change them.

This kind of support is one kind of external deadline you need to consider, but it's not the only kind. You need to consider events in the near to medium future that your book would be useful for or crucial to.

For example, I wrote this book so it would come out before my next scheduled brand shoot (and could be in the photos). If you're going to have a table at an upcoming business expo, you'd want copies of your book displayed for sale. If you're going to a big conference that's full of your ideal paying clients, you need to have your book done so you can hand it out instead of business cards. I know it's more expensive than a card, but which service provider are you more likely to follow-up with – one of the many who handed you a card, or the one who gave you a really useful book?

In addition to external deadlines, you need to consider internal/personal ones. For example, if you wanted to be a published author before a particular milestone birthday, do so – if you can without upending your whole life. Internal deadlines are only important to you, so you have to judge for yourself how much weight to give to them.

Putting your chosen approach into practice

Now that you know how you work and the time frame you're working in, it's time to put your work on your book into your diary.

If you're using an intensive model, resist the urge to simply block full days by writing 'work on book' in your diary. Instead, work in 2- to 3-hour blocks with planned breaks in between. For each block, set a task – for the drafting phase, use your outline to do this. Once you're in the revising/polishing phases, plan which chapter(s) you'll work on in each block.

Taking time to plan this early on will save time later – when you sit down to work, you won't be wasting time figuring out what you need to do next.

If you're using the little and often model, schedule two to four small blocks of time (either 4 half-hour blocks or 2 1-hour blocks). For each block, note which part of a chapter you're going to work on.

To begin with, plan a couple of days at a time. As you learn how much you can accomplish in each block, you'll be able to plan further ahead.

Whichever approach you're using, note big goals in your diary so you can see what you're working towards. What do I mean by *big goals*? The dates you're due to send your draft to someone:

- Your beta readers,

- Your editor,

- Your formatter, and

- Your publisher.

GET SUPPORT IN PLACE

NOW THAT YOU'RE CLEAR on how and when you're going to work on your book, we need to look at how you're going to get it out into the world!

Before you start writing, you need to get some support in place. Below, I'll discuss the most common types of support that authors need:

1. Beta readers

2. Editorial support

3. Book formatting/publication consultant

4. Cover design

Beta readers

What are beta readers, you ask? Beta readers are people who are very much like your ideal reader. You send your manuscript to them (usually) before you send it to your editor so you can find out whether or not you've written the book you wanted to write.

Your beta readers' job is not to fix your errors in punctuation, grammar, or spelling. Instead, they answer higher level questions like these (feel free to send your readers these exact questions, or write your own – just don't write too many, you don't want it to take ages for them to reply):

1. Does the book make sense?

2. Are there any points in the book where you feel like I've skipped a step or assumed you have knowledge that you don't?

3. Are there any points in the book where you feel like I'm explaining the obvious?

4. How is my tone? Overly familiar, too stuffy, just right?

5. What did you learn from the book?

6. Is there anything else you want to tell me so I can make the book as useful to my readers as possible?

You need feedback like this from people who have a lot in common with your target audience so you can make sure your book has hit the mark. It won't do any good to market a book written for professionals to an audience of novices, or vice versa.

Beta readers are also excellent sources of early reviews, which will help with your marketing, but more on that in chapters 14 and 16: 'Beta Readers' and 'Publish'.

How much do beta readers charge? Most writers find people in their networking or client groups who are happy to be beta readers for free, but I usually recommend at least sending them a physical copy of the book (with a handwritten thank you note) when it's in print. It's also nice to offer them a discount on your services or access to a pre-recorded course you've produced as an additional thank you.

While there are professional beta readers (whose charges vary according to their experience), I tend to steer my clients away from using them. Why? Because they aren't your ideal readers – unless, of course, you're writing a book about how to be a better beta reader.

You need to get your beta readers in place as soon as possible. When you send your draft to them, they'll need to have set aside time to read it and give you feedback. I usually recommend securing 4 to 6 beta readers, with the understanding that about half of your beta readers will have something come up that prevents them from following through and reading your draft. It's not their fault and shouldn't be cause for judging them, it's just that your book isn't as important to them as it is to you (or as their children, pets, businesses, etc. are to them).

Editorial support

All books need to go to a qualified editor before publication – running your text through a computer program that claims to catch and fix grammar errors is not sufficient. Human language is far too complex for machines to deal with effectively. Hiring a professional editor will help you avoid looking like an amateur and increase the chance that your book helps your readers. What level(s) of editing you need depends on what kind of writer you are.

If you didn't know that there were different levels of editing, you're not alone. Most people who aren't editors (or who don't work closely with editors) aren't aware of the different levels and don't really see a distinction between copyediting and proofreading.

What are the levels? Conventionally, from the big picture to minute details, they are as follows:

- Developmental editing – at this level, the editor works with the author to flesh out the high level structure of a book. This can involve identifying the topic and the book's particular take on that topic, a chapter level outline, and (occasionally) outlining individual chapters. You consult a developmental editor before you finish your first draft, and often before you even start your first draft.

- Copy (or line) editing – at this level, the editor makes sure spelling and punctuation rules are consistently applied. This does not mean that your book will read like it was written by a stuffy grammarian. A good copy editor will understand where to impose a 'rule' (grammar/usage rules aren't set in stone) and where to let your personal style stand – the decision will be guided by how easy the work will be for your target audience to understand. A copy editor will also make sure your tone/register is consistent throughout.

What does that mean? I'll use my own language as an example. I grew up in Oklahoma, but since I left there in 2001, I've earned a PhD from the University of California at Davis and spent more than 15 years living and teaching/coaching in the UK. As you might expect, the Okie drawl of my youth has long since disappeared, in most settings. When I've been spending time with my family (or talking to them on the phone), it comes back in my speech, so I'm more likely to ask, 'What are y'all doin' tonight?' than 'What are you doing tonight?' While the Okie drawl has never (yet) made it into my written language, I trust my copy editor to remove it for me and keep my readers from having the jarring experience of wondering why I turned over the writing of my work to someone else.

Finally, a copy editor will make sure your work flows from one section to the next, as well as within each section from one paragraph to the next. You send your typescript to your copy editor when you're almost ready to publish.

- Proofreading – a proofreader's job is to make sure that the copy editor's edits made it into the proofs (the pages of set type produced by a publisher). You send your proofs (from your publisher) and the copy edited manuscript to your proofreader before the book goes into production.

As I said above, these are the conventional uses of these terms, and as you can see especially in the definition of *proofreading*, they apply more to traditionally published books than to self-published ones.

If you're writing a book about how you help your clients, you almost certainly will **not** need a developmental editor. You know the process you use for your clients – let that process guide the shape of your book.

If you are writing in your native language, you'll probably need a proof-edit, not both a copy edit and a proofread.

What's a proof-edit and why isn't it in that list? *Proof-edit* isn't in that list because it's not a conventional term. Instead, it's the term I (and a few other editors) use to refer to what native speakers mean by 'proofread'. When I proof-edit a book, I do a light copy edit (check for consistency, style/grammar, and overall flow) and a check for errors – spelling, missing information, missing or incorrect punctuation.

If you're writing in your second (or third, fourth...) language, you'll need a bit more editorial support than a proof-edit. For non-native speakers, I'd recommend a full copy edit (by an editor with ample experience of working with non-native writers) and, if your budget allows, a proofread/proof-edit to make your manuscript as error free as possible.

When should you book your editor(s)? As soon as possible – like, put down this book and email your editor now (assuming you've worked out your deadlines, as discussed in chapter 6, 'Manage your time'). Editors' calendars get full quickly, and while it's possible to hire an editor at the last minute, it will cost you more if you do.

How much more? When clients ask me for tight turnarounds (meaning you're expecting me to rearrange my schedule to suit yours), I double or treble my price – so instead of charging £800 for a proof-edit of a 40-thousand-word book, I'd charge £1600 or £2400. If the turnaround is too tight for me to do the work to my standards, I simply don't take on the job.

Book formatting/publication consultant

Once you finish your book and address any issues raised by your beta readers and editor(s), you're ready to publish.

If you have no interest in learning how to do this yourself, you'll need to hire a publication consultant. When researching consultants, make sure you clearly understand who owns your intellectual property at the end of the process.

A reputable consultant understands that ISBN numbers are non-transferable – meaning they cannot give you a number 'for free' (as some large companies claim to do). If they buy the number on their account, in their name, they own it and the rights to any book it becomes attached to.

Also, a reputable consultant will make their money on the fee you pay for their publication services, not on your royalties. They will also have examples of previous clients' books for you to look at so you can see what quality you can expect for your book. Their pricing should be clear and free from hidden charges. Take your time when reading the contract, read reviews from past clients, and speak to past clients before you sign anything.

If you're willing to learn how to publish your book but have no interest in learning how to format its interior (this needs to be done before the file can be uploaded to Amazon and IngramSpark to publish the book), you'll need to hire a book formatter. A reputable formatter will have examples you can look at of their previous work. As with the publication consultant, their pricing should be clear and free from hidden charges. Take your time when reading the contract, read reviews from past clients, and speak to past clients before you sign anything.

Chapter 8

YOUR IDEAL READER

I KNOW, YOU'RE 8 chapters into a book on writing and you haven't started writing yet. Stick with me a little longer – you can't write a book that serves your reader if you don't know who your reader is.

As writers, it's all too easy to make the book about us – after all, it's our lives that are centred on it while we're writing. But we don't really matter so much once the book is published.

After publication the book doesn't need a writer anymore, but it will always need readers.

While you're working on your book you need to keep one (fictional) ideal reader in mind. If you've been keeping a demographic group in mind, the idea of focusing on just one reader may be a bit scary but hear me out.

Your book is not a social media ad

If you've ever created an ad on social media, you've used demographics to determine your audience – you've focused on people grouped by commonalities like location, age, gender, annual income, and common interests.

This approach is great for an ad (that's why the major social media platforms use it). Why does it work for an ad? Because it's a short piece of writing (or video) that's only asking for a few moments of your audience's time. Ads only need to connect on one tiny point to get that attention.

Your book, however, is asking for a longer time commitment and a much more personal, even intimate connection. Almost no one is going to devote hours to reading a generalised message created for the masses. What will they commit to reading? A book that speaks directly to them on a personal level.

This doesn't mean you need to write a different book for every reader. You just need to write a book that speaks to a person, not a demographic group.

How does it work?

When you write to a person, you write more naturally than you do when you're trying to please the masses. There's a reason this old saying has been around so long (and has been attributed to everyone from Aesop to Ricky Gervais): 'When you try to please everyone, you please no one.'

When you write to the masses, you water down your message to the point that you don't say much of anything. When you write to one person, you open the possibility for meaningful communication. By doing that, you make it possible for lots of different kinds of people to connect with you, your book, and your message.

Don't believe me? Let me tell you a story.

One of my clients, Abbie Broad, author of *Does It Really Need to Be This Hard?* (2020), wrote her book to a British woman who lives with her husband and their children. Abbie's ideal reader is 42 years old and is starting her business now that her children are old enough to not need all of her attention all day every day (they're in school). When Abbie sent the draft to her cover designer, a German man in his early 30s who wasn't married and didn't have children, she thought he'd have a quick look through the opening pages to get a feel for the book before he created a few sample covers for her to choose from.

Imagine her surprise when he texted her the next morning to say he'd gotten so wrapped up in her book, he'd stayed up into the wee hours to read the whole thing!

Why was a man who had precious little in common with Abbie's reader so engrossed by her book? Because Abbie's an engaging writer. Her writing is engaging mostly because she writes to one person who needs to hear her message. By making her book relevant and necessary to one ideal reader, she makes it so for lots of different kinds of readers.

When I wrote to Abbie to ask her permission to use this story (see chapter 12, 'Polish', for more on how to use other people's material responsibly and ethically), she said:

The feedback I've had from so many who read it is "it's like you're in my head Abbie... and you know exactly how I'm feeling". (personal communication, 23/08/2022)

This quality is what makes a book successful. Keep reading to find out how you can do this, too!

Get to know your ideal reader

The first step in writing a book to one ideal reader is figuring out who that reader is and what makes her (him or them) tick.

I've created a worksheet to help you do this. You'll find it on pages 73—79 or you can download it here: https://ewc.coach/ready-to-publish-resources/

Here's mine from my preparation for writing this book:

Ideal reader's name: Jo

Age: 45

Family/living situation: Jo lives with her husband of 20 years and their 3 cats. Her husband is a lawyer who specialises in property law. They live in Southampton. She grew up in Cornwall; her parents and sister still live there.

Interests: Jo has eclectic tastes in music (rock, blues, country, jazz, baroque, classical, etc.) and books (everything from bodice rippers to classic novels – so long as it has a compelling narrative). She's mostly vegetarian and loves to cook – she collects cookbooks and reads them for inspiration (she rarely follows a recipe exactly as it's written).

Where do they hang out on social media? She uses Facebook to connect with old friends and family, but she spends most of her time on LinkedIn and Instagram for her business.

Where do they hang out in real life? Jo loves curling up with a good book on the sofa with her cats and husband. When she goes out she prefers independent cafés, microbreweries, casual restaurants.

Profession (what do they do, for how long, etc.): Jo is a business coach who's been helping new entrepreneurs get clear on their offerings and messages for the last 15 years.

What brings your reader to your book: She started her book about 5 years ago, but it got lost in the chaos of Covid. Since then, it's been gathering digital dust on her hard drive. She really wants to finish it – it's getting embarrassing to have to keep telling her business friends that it's not out yet. She's also annoyed with herself for not finishing it – to the point that she's getting occasional bouts of imposter syndrome, even though she thought she'd dealt with that a decade ago.

What (about the problem you solve) keeps your reader up at night? Jo worries that her book isn't good enough – though she's been coaching for years and has had lots of excellent reviews from clients, and she'd never admit this even to herself, she still has a touch of imposter syndrome when it comes to declaring herself expert enough to publish her book. This fear has kept her from getting the support she needs to finally finish and publish it.

She's also worried about how her business and life will change when she becomes more visible – she's a talented public speaker but has been told she will only get on the really big stages after she hits publish. Being that visible is scary – what changes will it bring to her work/life balance? Her husband is supportive, but how will he feel if she actually starts earning more than he does? What will that do to their relationship?

How much does your reader know about your field/topic? Jo's a reasonably confident writer. Like most coaches, she's blogged on and off since starting her business, but this is her first book, so she doesn't know all the ins and outs of finishing it and getting it out into her readers' hands.

How is your reader likely to use your book? Is it an instruction manual they can use for reference, or do they need to read the whole thing? Or something in between? This book is an 'in between' kind of book – Jo will benefit from reading the whole thing before she starts work on her own manuscript, but she'll likely need to dip in and out of it while she's working to remind her of the details covered in it.

To this point, the worksheet probably hasn't had any surprises for you. For the most part, these early questions are the kinds of questions you're used to seeing in the various exercises you've no doubt done to get to know your ideal paying client.

The rest of the worksheet might seem odd if it's the first time you've considered these issues for an ideal reader/client, but it is well worth your time to finish this exercise. The later questions get into how your ideal reader thinks about the world she lives in. This will help you differentiate between people who would be a good fit for working with you/reading your book and those who wouldn't.

Remember, you don't have to please everyone. In fact, irritating some people who don't share your values is actually a good thing for you as an author and as a business owner.

So, take a deep breath and try to accept that not everyone is going to love your book. Also, if you can help the 'wrong' people see that it's the wrong book for them early on, you'll save everyone a lot of time and hassle.

Without further ado, let's look at how your reader thinks:

Did they vote in the last election? If so, for whom?
Yes, she always votes for the most progressive candidate available.

Do they practice a religion? Which one? If not, why not? She doesn't. She's what a lot of people would describe as 'spiritual', though she hates that label – while she connects with Spirit/Source/the Universe as and when she feels called to do so, she doesn't adhere to any one spiritual/religious tradition. She finds some truth in several types of spiritual practice but rejects people/groups who claim to have found 'the' truth.

How do they feel about major political issues? – Brexit, Johnson's premiership, the rise of Trumpism, ... Like most people, she pays more attention to political issues that have a direct impact on her daily life and has strong opinions on British and European politics – for example, she thinks Brexit was a terrible idea from the start and has been handled badly by the Tories. She's aware of and has opinions about many issues that aren't so close to home (Russia's invasion of Ukraine, Trump's various escapades); as in her domestic politics, she tends to be a progressive.

How do they feel about major social justice issues? – Black Lives Matter, Women's rights, Trans rights, ... If she had the time and resources, she'd be an activist. She's frequently infuriated by stories about people in power stomping (too often literally) on those without power. Nevertheless, she often feels powerless to do more than rage against injustices.

How do they feel about themselves? Are they happy with their body? Do they see themselves as smart and capable, or are they always worried they're not good enough? Jo has fairly solid self-esteem, but like most people she wobbles from time to time. Most often her wobbles happen when she is, or is about to be, more visible/vocal than usual. For example, while she's generally comfortable in her own skin and confident in her knowledge and abilities, when she's preparing for a speaking event (especially an in person event), she notices little doubts creeping in. For the most part, she's good at seeing these for what they are (nerves) and carrying on despite them, but she has a harder time doing that when she's faced with an entirely new situation – like publishing her first book.

How do they feel about their relationships? Jo is happy and secure in her important relationships. Like many people, her 20s were spent learning to set and maintain healthy boundaries both with family members and with friends and romantic partners. Now that she's a bit older and more experienced, she's able to maintain her relationships by communicating her needs clearly and by actually listening to the needs of others.

How did they get to where they are now? What obstacles have they overcome? What are their achievements? Jo started coaching after having taught secondary school for more than 10 years. She loved teaching, but she loathed all the pointless admin, government monitoring exercises, and office politics. Once her husband's law practice was established enough to provide some financial security, she took the decision to leave teaching and start her own business. After spending a few months considering her options, she decided to train as a business coach – coaching would give her many of the things she loved about teaching (watching her clients/students develop and overcome their limiting beliefs) without the bureaucracy that goes along with working in a school. Her main obstacle in her business life has been developing the confidence to believe she can and is allowed to do things her own way – it's taken a while to overcome the habits of thought ingrained in her during her years in the school system. Her achievements are all the students/clients she's helped over the years, as well as a handful of small, but important to her, business awards.

What was their childhood like? How do they now feel about the people who were around when they were growing up? Jo grew up in a two-parent household with one younger sister. As an adult, she has good relationships with all three, though her parents, especially her mother, will always wonder about her decision to leave the perceived security of her teaching job for her coaching career. She has come to accept that they're never going to completely understand, and it's not her job to make them see her life as she sees it.

Hopefully after reading all of that you feel like you sort of know Jo. You should have an idea of where she came from, what sort of life she's had, and have a good idea of where she is now and how she's feeling about her book.

You may be wondering why you needed to worry about things like where she grew up, how she feels about people she lived with, what kind of relationships she has, or how she feels about herself and her appearance. You need to understand these things about your reader so you can understand more about how they feel about the thing you're helping them with.

If you look at my answer to the last question on the worksheet about how Jo feels about her parents, I say that 'She has come to accept that they are never going to completely understand' the decisions she's made and that 'it's not her job to make them see her life as she sees it'. It's this kind of realisation she's going to have to come to about her book and her future readers before she can hit publish and let her book go – she needs to see that she's never going to make all of the people who might read her book love it, and it's not her job to do that. Her job is to write the best book she can to help the people who need it and who will love it.

Now look at the sentence before that one, where I said that Jo knows that 'her parents, especially her mother, will always wonder about her decision to leave the perceived security of her teaching job for her coaching career' – *they* saw her teaching job as secure, and *they* struggle to understand why she has chosen to set out to do something completely new.

She's not internalising their fears, but she is fully recognising what she's accomplished. The experience of having done something completely new by leaving the teaching job that she trained for and that she did well in for a number of years to go set up her successful coaching practice, despite her parents' reservations, will help her in her endeavour to become a published author. Once she can map the experience of leaving her career to set up her business onto the new experience of finishing and publishing her book, she'll be fully equipped for the work she needs to do to finish the book and for the changes that having the book out will make to her business and her life.

That should make it clearer how understanding these bits about the psychology of your ideal reader will help you write your book in such a way that you'll get them to come to the conclusions they need to in order to achieve the transformation your book delivers. You'll need your reader to connect with your authorial voice enough to reach these conclusions on their own because it's not the sort of thing you can just tell them to do.

For example, I can't just tell Jo that she needs to see that writing her book is just like setting up her coaching practice. Even if Jo were a real person and I had an in person conversation with her, that statement wouldn't result in her instantly believing she can publish a successful book. Why not? Because her first reaction would be to list all the ways this situation isn't like her career change.

Instead of telling her what conclusion to reach, I need to show her what the steps are and make her believe that she can take them and get them done. As she builds that self-belief, she'll start seeing parallels to other obstacles she's overcome.

If you're reading this and thinking this is all very meta (no, not the way Zuckerberg uses the word) with me telling you, a reader who's already sort of identifying with Jo in a lot of ways, that I can't just tell you how to do these things, you're right; it is. If you go on to finish reading this book and publish yours, you may someday think back on this paragraph and realise I was right. I couldn't just tell you publishing your book is like some other experience you've had, but by helping you develop the skills you need to do it; you've applied what you learned from a previous trial to this one.

I hope you've set aside some time now or in the near future to go through the worksheet on pages 73—79 so that you can get to know your reader and their concerns. Doing that will help you understand what they need from you and from your book. Getting to know your reader will also make writing your book much easier because it will be like you're talking to them as a friend – and while writing a book may (sometimes) sound scary, there's nothing scary about having a conversation with a friend about how you can help them solve a problem.

What does your reader need?

Now that you have a good idea of who your ideal reader is, it's time to figure out what they need from your book.

So that you don't fall into the trap of trying to force your existing draft to fit with your reader's needs, resist the urge to open and read what you've already written. Instead, take out a blank sheet of paper – ideally one that doesn't have any lines on it – and a colourful writing instrument, like a crayon or brightly coloured pen.

I know this sounds a bit weird but stick with me for a minute. When we write on lined paper in blue or black ink, it takes us back to school days, and we start judging everything we write. If you wrote on lined paper in red ink, it would look like your teacher had bled all over your page – that's just going to send you into a panic. When we use unlined paper and brightly coloured writing instruments, our brains don't see it as work. This means we don't get scared that we're going to be judged. Getting rid of the fear of judgement allows us to just be creative. That's what you need to be doing for the next few minutes.

On your sheet of paper list the problems your ideal reader has that you might be able to solve. Don't worry about the order you put them in, just list ideas until you run out of things to list.

To keep this exercise from taking longer than it needs to set a timer for about 15 to 20 minutes. That gives you enough time to give it the consideration and needs, but not so much that it becomes a time waster in and of itself.

When your timer goes off, put the piece of paper to the side and go do something else for at least an hour. This will give your brain time to think about what you've been listing in the background, without you worrying over it. Your brain's actually better off doing this without your conscious input. Why? Because your conscious mind has its own priorities that will get in the way of your unconscious doing what it does best – processing and filtering information.

When you go back to your list, read it through and pay attention to which item on the list jumps out at you as the most important problem for you to solve for your reader right now. That doesn't discount the urgency or importance of the other problems, rather it shows you which problem you're most invested in right now. Identifying which one you're most invested in is going to make finishing your book a lot easier.

Not convinced? Think about how kids respond to food – most kids are pretty quick to finish things they like, like ice cream, but they can take ages over a vegetable they're not too sure about, like broccoli. You don't want your book to be broccoli (I have nothing against broccoli – it's one of my favourite veggies – but a lot of people can't stand it, hence its use here).

Once you've chosen which problem you're going to solve for your reader, you're ready to start narrowing down your topic to one that can be dealt with within one book.

Let's have a look at the list of ideas I came up with for my ideal reader Jo.

- She needs help learning how to use her book to promote her business.

- She needs help understanding the technical aspects of how to publish her book including formatting, editing, and cover design.

- She needs help finding and polishing the book hidden in her copious notes, transcripts, and draft pages.

- She needs help developing the mindset of an author.

- She needs help seeing that the draft she has started is worth publishing and will be useful to future readers.

- She needs an understanding of how her book can work in and with her business.

That's enough to be getting on with. As you can see, all these problems are related to writing – there's no point listing all of the possible problems your reader might have, only list the ones you might possibly be able to help them with. Since I'm a writing coach, I've focused on writing! Since you're reading this book, it should come as no surprise that the one problem that jumped out for me was, 'She needs help finding and polishing the book hidden in her copious notes, transcripts, and draft pages.'

You may now be looking at the table of contents of this book and thinking that I've dealt with a lot of other problems, but here I am saying your book should only solve one problem. That's still true, a book can only solve one problem in full. For this one, the big problem that it solves is how to sort through the existing draft to find a publishable book, revise that book, and get it ready for publication.

The other problems I touch on, like learning to see yourself as an author and understanding how to use your book in your business, aren't dealt with in as much detail, but they're so closely related to the main problem that I couldn't leave them out altogether.

Ideal Reader

Name:

Age:

Family/living situation:

Interests:

Where do they hang out on social media?

Where do they hang out in real life?

Profession (what do they do, for how long, etc.):

What brings your reader to your book?

What (about the problem you solve) keeps your reader up at night?

How much does your reader know about your field/topic?

How is your reader likely to use your book? Is it an instruction manual they can use for reference, or do they need to read the whole thing? Or is it something in between?

Did they vote in the last election? If so, for whom?

Do they practise a religion? Which one? If not, why not?

How do they feel about major political issues? — Brexit, Johnson's premiership, the rise of Trumpism, ...

How do they feel about major social justice issues? — Black Lives Matter, Women's rights, Trans rights, ...

How do they feel about themselves? Are they happy with their body? Do they see themselves as smart and capable, or are they always worried they're not good enough?

How do they feel about their relationships?

How did they get to where they are now? What obstacles have they overcome? What are their achievements?

What was their childhood like? How do they feel about the people who were around when they were growing up?

Chapter 9

FOCUS AND OUTLINE YOUR BOOK

I N THIS CHAPTER WE'RE going to use the topic you chose in the previous one as the foundation for your book. By the end of the chapter you'll have an idea of the structure and length of your book!

Statement of argument

Now you need to craft your statement of argument. Your statement of argument is a one sentence statement of the main point of your book.

Remember, the broad topic we're working with here is: 'Jo needs help finding and polishing the book hidden in her copious notes, transcripts, and draft pages.'

Just as when you create materials for your coaching programmes, courses, or talks, when you're focusing the topic of your book, you need to start with the end goal in mind. For my reader, that end goal is to finish and publish their book.

When new writers craft their first statement of argument, their tendency is to go too broad. Why?

Because they want their books to appeal to as many people as possible – as discussed in chapter 8. So you might be tempted to write something like this: *Some people write books based on material they developed for other purposes.*

It is true that some people write books based on material developed for other purposes, but that's not an arguable statement – it's a statement of fact. You can't really write a book based on a statement of fact. If you were to try to use this sentence as your foundation, what would be in the book? A list of people who have done that? Such a book is hardly going to grab your readers' attention – and it certainly won't solve their problem.

A better one would be this: 'You can easily write a book based on material you developed for other purposes.' This is arguably true, but I'd have some work to do to convince you of it.

Book outline

Your statement of argument is the foundation for your book, and now you're going to use it to create your book outline!

Start by writing your statement of argument at the top of an unlined sheet of paper using a brightly coloured writing implement (if you need a reminder of why this matters, see page 68).

Next, set a timer for 30 minutes and list all the questions you might need to answer to convince your reader that your statement of argument is true. Here's some of what I came up with for this book:

'You can easily write a book based on material you developed for other purposes.'

- How do you know you can write a book?

- How do you know if the material you've created is worth putting into a book?

- How do you know if anyone will read your book?

- How do you format your book for publishing?

- How do you find the focus of your book in all those pages and pages of transcripts/drafts/etc.?

- How do you edit your own work?

- How will you find time to write your book?

- Will this work for any book, or only certain types?

- Will writing a book be worth it for you? For your business?

- How long will it take?

- How do you turn what you have into reader-friendly material?

When the timer goes off, or you run out of questions to ask about your statement of argument, put your list aside for at least an hour. As I explained when you were working out what your ideal reader needs from your book (see page 69), you need to leave your unconscious to do its thing. While that's going in the background, you can do something else – go for a walk, have a nap, clean your kitchen, have a coaching call, etc.

When you go back to your list, cross out any questions that are beyond the scope of your book and put the remaining questions in a logical order. Don't stress about getting it exactly right, your chapter order will change as you work on your book.

When you're happy with your outline, take a picture of it – that way you'll still have it, even if your coffee gets knocked over on the page!

A note on length

It's usually at the outlining stage that writers start worrying about how long their book should be. I can't give you a clear cut answer to that. Sorry, I know that's not what you wanted to hear.

To determine how long your book should be, you need to look at your topic and your reader.

For a book like mine, which is on a topic that makes lots of readers anxious, it needs to be short and to the point. If you're worried about tackling a seemingly big job like finishing your book, you're not going to be encouraged by first having to read a massive book about how to do it. That's why I keep my books about writing between 25k and 35k words. I don't want the work of finishing your book to feel too heavy (and thus too hard) to manage before you even start.

I've had clients who incorporated portions of their life stories into their books to illustrate the points they were making about the kinds of coaching they offer. These books come in between 60k and 100k words. Readers who are engaged in the narrative of a person's life want to know more. So go into as much detail as your reader needs in the narrative sections and keep the coaching/advice sections tightly focused and on the short side.

If you're writing a book that's a mixture of personal narrative and coaching exercises, make sure it's easy for your reader to find the coaching exercises when they return to your book – either put them at the ends of chapters in clearly marked sections or in chapters of their own at the end of the book!

I've also had clients write books to help their readers understand and cope with health issues. When people are looking for information to help them manage their health they want all the relevant information, and they want it in an easy to use and understand format. If you're writing about such a topic, you'll likely end up with at least 50k words (and could easily go on to 80k or more). Your readers will welcome the wealth of information so long as you present it in easy to understand terms – in other words, make sure a layperson can easily read it.

If you're still not sure roughly how long your book should be, go to a large bookstore, find the section that stocks books similar to what you're writing, and look at books by a few authors you admire. Are they mostly slim volumes or chunky tomes? That gives you something to aim for.

Now it's time to stop worrying about how long your book should be and get started on getting it ready to publish!

Chapter 10

CHECK YOUR DRAFT AGAINST YOUR BOOK OUTLINE

NOW THAT YOU HAVE a book outline, it's time to move your existing material into it so you can see how much drafting you still need to do.

What do I mean by 'existing material'? This can take many forms, including (but not limited to):

- A document in which you wrote part of your book

- Transcripts from your recorded course

- Transcripts from your recorded talks or workshops

- Notes you took before or after coaching sessions/programmes

If your existing material is on paper (and you don't have it digitally), your first task is to scan each page and save it as a PDF. That way, you still have it, even if something happens to one or more of the pages as you physically cut and paste it into your outline.

If you've written on both sides, you'll also need to photocopy the reverse pages because you'll be physically cutting and pasting chunks of text – that won't work if the front side of page 5 belongs in chapter 3, but the reverse side goes in chapter 7.

If your existing material is in a digital document (Word doc, Google doc, etc.), save an extra copy and give it a name like 'original draft – do not touch'. That way, if something happens to the file while you're working on it, you've got a backup. Save the one you're working from as 'original draft – working copy'.

Time to move text

Paper and scissors: clear a table or other large work surface. Write each question from your outline on a sticky note and number them. Stick the outline notes to your worksurface.

Then start reading and moving text. As you find paragraphs or pages that belong in a particular chapter, cut them and put them under that sticky note.

When you're done, type your draft as it is before moving on to the next step.

Digital draft: open a new document and name it something like 'book draft 1 – date'. Saving your draft with the date each time you work on it makes it easier to revert to earlier drafts should you need to do so. It also makes it easy to know which version is most up to date.

Next, type your outline into the document and format the question for each chapter as a level 1 header (in Word, you can do this from the home tab under 'Styles'; in Google docs, use the pull down menu in the toolbar). If you're thinking, 'you're not supposed to use header 1 that way', you're right – we're doing so here because that's what the formatting software will need to see when you (or your book formatter) upload it for publication.

Then, start reading and moving text by cutting it out of your 'working copy' and pasting it under the appropriate heading in your 'book draft'.

What about the stuff that doesn't fit?

You're likely to have some material in your original draft that doesn't really fit anywhere in your new outline. Don't try to force it to fit. Instead, save it for another project.

Find the gaps

It's possible, even likely, you have sections that don't have any material in them at all – those are obvious gaps.

To find the less obvious ones, you'll need to do the following:

1. Outline each chapter. To do this, answer the question for that chapter from your book outline in a single sentence. This is your statement of argument for that chapter. Once you have that, list the questions you'll need to answer to convince your reader it's true. For most chapters, aim for 3 to 5 questions. But be aware that some chapters need to be short and sweet, while others will need to be a bit longer. Don't stress about trying to make them uniform in length.

2. Type the questions/headings for your chapter outline into your draft – use Heading 2 for these. You'll change (at least some of) these to shorter headings when you polish your chapter. For now, leave them as questions.

3. Save a copy of your draft.

4. Move the material in that chapter into the appropriate sections. Whether you cut and paste within your working document or you use two separate documents is up to you – do what feels best. Whatever you do, save your work frequently.

When you finish moving material into your chapter outline, you should be able to identify gaps within chapters. Once you've done that, move on to the next step.

Fill the gaps

Your task now is to quickly draft the missing chapters or subsections.

When I say: 'quickly draft', I really do mean it. Your first draft's only job is to be done.

Writing 'good' first drafts is a waste of your time. When I explain the writing process to my clients, I compare it to clearing out your wardrobe (hence the name of my podcast, Wardrobes and Writing).[1]

The first step in clearing out your wardrobe is chucking all the clothes in the wardrobe onto your bed so you can see what you have. It would be a waste of time to tailor a jacket you haven't worn in years to fit your body now before you even decide if you want to keep it. Likewise, it's silly to spend time worrying about tiny issues like word choice, sentence structure, and punctuation for sentences you're not sure you're going to keep.

It's also silly to spend time at this stage trying to get references (like the ones below to Lamott and Baty) just right or internal references (like when I refer back to previous chapters, sections, or pages). Instead, just highlight the section that needs information and insert something like ?? or ** (aka punctuation/symbols you wouldn't normally use) to make it easy to use the find

---

1. You can learn more about my podcast and subscribe to it here: https://ewc.coach/speaker-podcaster/

tool (ctrl+f on PCs or cmd+f on Macs) to find all of them when you're polishing your text.

If your inner perfectionist is cringing at the thought of writing a messy draft, take a deep breath and promise her that your eyes are the only ones that will ever see it.

Still not convinced? Have a look at chapter 3 from Anne Lamott's *Bird by Bird* (1995) – it's called 'Shitty First Drafts'.[2] Chris Baty also discusses writing this way in *No Plot? No Problem!: A Low-Stress, High-Velocity Guide to Writing a Novel in 30 Days* (2014).

If you're still struggling to write quickly and without going back to polish as you go, try using the speech to text tool in your word processor (both Word and Google docs have this feature) or an app like otter.ai – I used these tools for much of the first draft of this book, and it saved me a lot of time.

Whatever method you use – fill those gaps quickly. Before you know it, you'll have a full first draft!

---

2. Excerpt from 'Shitty First Drafts': https://wrd.as.uky.edu/sites/default/files/1-Shitty%20First%20Drafts.pdf

Chapter 11

FIRST REVISION: BIG PICTURE ISSUES

C ONGRATULATIONS ON YOUR FIRST full draft! Now we start making it prettier!

If your inner perfectionist was miffed about being on the side-lines while you were drafting, she'll be happier now. She gets to come back to play, a bit.

Why only *a bit*? Your first revision is *not* about polishing your sentences (that comes a little later in the process). Instead, it's about bigger picture issues:

1. Chapter/section focus: does each chapter (or section within a chapter) do what it sets out to do?

2. Paragraph focus: does each paragraph have one (and only one) point?

3. Transitions: are there logical transitions between sections and chapters?

Check chapter and section focus

To check whether each chapter and section does what it sets out to do, work through these steps:

1. Read the statement of argument for that chapter.

2. Read the chapter and mark any passages that veer off topic.

3. Look at your subsections – does the material under each one stay tightly focused? If not, mark passages that veer off topic.

4. Go back to the marked passages and either refocus them or move them to where they fit better (this might be to a 'to be used later' file – don't delete anything; just move it to another document).

Check paragraph focus

If you tend to have 5 or more paragraphs per page (of typed, single-spaced A4), your paragraphs are probably fairly focused. Spend your time looking at longer paragraphs. Make sure each one makes only one point.

If you need help with paragraph structure, you can use this format (please note that not all paragraphs do – or should – follow it; it's just an example):

- Topic sentence – state the point of the paragraph

- Evidence sentence(s) – offer evidence to prove that point

- Analysis sentence(s) – show how the evidence proves the point made in the topic sentence.

How long should a paragraph be?

There's no magic answer to this question.

When we read books (whether we read paperbacks or eBooks on our smart phones), we (unconsciously) expect paragraphs to be of varying lengths. Paragraph length in a book is determined by the sense of what you're saying, not by what it looks like on a screen. In your book, you don't need to fear multi-sentence paragraphs because they aren't going to look like a wall of text on the page.

Writers, usually without even thinking about it, let their medium dictate their paragraph length. When you're writing for social media, you probably use very short paragraphs (1 to 2 sentences). In your blog posts, you likely use slightly longer ones. In your book, they can be longer still – but this doesn't mean they all have to be.

Use short paragraphs for emphasis and longer ones for deeper issues.

See what I did there – the short paragraph above emphasises my point and stands out because it has white space around it. Visually, that lets the reader pause (not a noticeable pause, but an important one all the same) to process the message. Inserting such a short paragraph in the middle of a discussion of paragraph length both breaks up the rather dry material and drives home the point.

As you consider your paragraph structure, you can use this technique to emphasise important points. But be careful. If you make every point you make into a short, punchy paragraph, they won't stand out. The emphasis will be lost in what will look like a list. In short: use the technique sparingly.

Check transitions

While reading your book, your reader will need some signposting to help them follow its logic. This doesn't have to be elaborate, but you do need to take a little time over it by following these three steps:

1. Read the last sentence or two of a section/chapter.

2. Read the first sentence of the next section/chapter.

3. Ask if it's clear why one needs to follow the next. If it's not clear, make it clear.

Example 1: In the opening section of this chapter, I list the three types of bigger picture issues covered in it:

1. Chapter/section focus: does each chapter (or section within a chapter) do what it sets out to do?

2. Paragraph focus: does each paragraph have one (and only one) point?

3. Transitions: are there logical transitions between sections and chapters?

The section headings then pick up on this language: *Check chapter sections and focus*, *Check paragraph focus*, and *Check transitions*. That's all my readers need to follow the logic of this chapter!

Example 2: Transitions don't have to be governed by numbered lists! Look at the end of chapter 10 and the beginning of this one:

> Before you know it, you'll have a full first draft! (p. 96)

> Congratulations on your first full draft! (p. 97)

It's clear from these sentences that in chapter 10 you're finishing your first draft, while in chapter 11, you're moving on to the next step.

As these examples illustrate, transitions don't have to be difficult, but you do need them. Why do you need them? So your reader understands where they are in the book. They need to know how what they're reading now relates to what they've read before.

Now that you have clearly focused chapters, chapter sections, and paragraphs and you've checked the logic between sections and chapters, you're ready to move on to the next step – Polish!

Chapter 12

SECOND REVISION: POLISH

Y OU'RE READY TO POLISH your writing. This is the moment your inner perfectionist has been waiting for: she gets full rein – for a while.

As you polish your text in preparation for sending it to your beta readers, you need to keep a couple of things in mind:

1. It doesn't need to be error free. You'll be sending your draft to a professional proofreader/editor when you get it back from your beta readers.

2. It's impossible to proofread your own work. You're far too clever for your own good. How? Your brain will read what you meant to type, not what's actually on the page/screen. So obsessing over catching every little thing is a waste of time.

While it is impossible to proofread your own work, there are some things you can do to make the text easier for your beta readers to read. In this chapter, we'll start by looking at chapter titles and subheadings, then at permissions and referencing, and finally at sentence level issues.

Chapter titles

Are all of your chapter titles still in the form of questions from your outline? I thought so.

Using questions as chapter titles isn't necessarily a problem. Whether you change yours or not is up to you.

If you're writing a book on the seven big questions you need to answer before changing career, and the titles of your seven main chapters are in the form of questions, that's great. Your reader will expect to open to the table of contents and see those questions.

However, if all or part of your book is dedicated to detailing a process for doing something, seeing a list of questions might be disconcerting for a reader who's looking for the answers/instructions. Or if all or part of your book is about your personal story, seeing a list of questions would just be confusing for your reader. For these types of books, seriously consider changing all or some of your chapter titles to topical statements or key words.

Subheadings

As you revise your subheadings, think about how your reader will use them. When we read narrative nonfiction, like memoirs and biographies, we don't like or need a lot of subsections. Why? When we read narrative nonfiction, as when we read novels, we tend to read all the words, rather than skim through looking for particular information. If your book (or chapter) is a narrative (not a how-to), it's better to have no or few subsections. If that's what you're writing, delete all or most of the headings you put in as your chapter outline – they've served their purpose.

When we read how-to books (or chapters), like the one you're reading now, subheadings are really useful. If you need to find a section later and remember what chapter it's in, skimming the subheadings can help you find what part of that chapter you need.

You also need fairly frequent subheadings in how-to books. Again, this is about how we read such books. Your reader might not read your book from start to finish. Instead, they might open to a particular chapter, read the chapter title and the subheadings, and then decide whether to read the whole chapter, or only the parts that are relevant to what they're looking for.

Whether your subheadings remain in the form of questions or not is entirely up to you. Subheadings generally are not included in tables of contents, so there's no risk of your reader being overwhelmed by a list of questions.

Permissions and referencing

Remember on page 95 when I said you should highlight text that needs an external reference and insert something like ?? or ** to make them easy to find? This is when you go through your draft to put those references in (for internal references to previous pages/chapters, you'll need to wait until your book is formatted).

Do not skip this step – skipping it could destroy your credibility and possibly land you in legal trouble.

As an author, it is your responsibility to make sure you use whatever information you use in your book responsibly. What does it mean to use information responsibly? It means to give credit where credit is due. If you paraphrase, summarise, or quote a source, obviously you need to cite that source. The purpose of the citation is both to give credit to the original author and to allow your reader to go read the original for themselves.

For example, whenever you quote a sentence from somebody else's book, you're taking it out of context to some degree. In that case, your reader might want to make sure they agree with how you've presented the sentence, or they might want to follow up and read the entire book for themselves. In such a situation, your citation has served two purposes: giving credit to the original author and allowing your reader to decide how much background reading they want to do on your topic.

The importance of giving credit to the original author is both just common courtesy – nobody likes having their stuff stolen – and a legal obligation. You can get into legal trouble if you steal someone else's intellectual property.

Quoting someone without citing them is theft.

There's really no difference between stealing somebody's car and stealing their ideas, except, I suppose, it's easier to prove ownership of a car. Since I assume you don't want to end up having ugly e-mail exchanges with lawyers, and you certainly don't want to end up in a courthouse over intellectual property theft, make sure you site every publication that you quote.

You should also cite other, less formal sources. If you look back at chapter 8, 'Your ideal reader', you'll see that I cite personal correspondence with Abbie Broad. While suing me over not citing such correspondence would likely be too expensive to be worth her while, it's courteous to Abbie as a person to give her credit when I use her words and ideas.

You can see on page 55, I've presented the Abbie's words as a quotation – by setting them apart as a block quotation and then putting the citation in the parentheses after the quotation. That citation explains that the quotation is our personal correspondence from 23 August 2022. That's all you need to do if you're citing a fairly informal, private source like an e-mail, unpublished letter, text exchange, or conversation.

If you're citing a published work (a book, website, article, newsletter, or social media post), you need to give enough information that your reader can get back to the source (if at all possible).

For digital sources, the easiest way to do that is to give your reader a DOI (digital object identifier). If your source doesn't have a DOI, give a stable URL – you need to make sure it's a stable URL or you're going to have trouble publishing the eBook version of your book; also, it's irritating for readers of your book if they go to a website you mentioned only to find a broken link.

For print sources (books or print media like articles in magazines or newspapers), it is usually enough to give the following details:

- the author's name,

- the title of the article or book that you're citing,

- the title of the original publication if part of a larger publication, and

- the date of publication.

You can go a bit further and give the place of publication, which is generally what academics do.

In addition to citing your sources in the body of your text, it's nice for readers to have a works cited list at the end of the book that includes all of your published (not personal correspondence/conversations) sources. I always include these to make it easier for readers who may remember that I referred to a book that looked interesting, but who can't remember in which chapter I mentioned it.

For how to format these things, you can use your own system (just make sure it's consistent and includes all the important information (in the list above). If you'd rather use an established system, you'll find an overview of Harvard APA,[1] MLA,[2] and Chicago (CMOS)[3] in the footnotes. Alternatively, Google the name of the referencing system of your choice to find a free guide to using it.

Sentence level revisions

This is the part your inner perfectionist has been waiting for – now, you get to go through your text and fix the punctuation and grammar (to the best of your ability – remember your professional proofreader/editor has yet to go through your manuscript).

---

1. Purdue OWL overview of Harvard APA:

   https://owl.purdue.edu/owl/research_and_citation
   /apa_style/apa_formatting_and_style_guide/refer
   ence_list_basic_rules.html

2. Purdue OWL overview of MLA:

   https://owl.purdue.edu/owl/research_and_citation
   /mla_style/mla_formatting_and_style_guide/mla_
   general_format.html

3. Purdue OWL overview of Chicago Manual of Style:

   https://owl.purdue.edu/owl/research_and_citation
   /chicago_manual_17th_edition/cmos_formatting_
   and_style_guide/chicago_manual_of_style_17th_e
   dition.html

As I said at the beginning of this chapter, you're not going to catch all the errors because you're too clever for your own good. That said, there are some things you can do to increase your effectiveness.

1. Read each chapter from the last sentence to the first – this will help you catch typos (by making reading something you have to think about doing) but won't help if you're worried about the overall flow of the chapter. As above, highlight sentences that need work. This is even more effective if you change the font or background colour or zoom in to 200% (or bigger) – basically anything you can do to make your text look different to how it did when you wrote it.

2. Read your book out loud yourself – for some reason we're more likely to read what's actually on the page when we do this than when we

---

4. You'll find instructions for doing this in Google Docs here: Google Docs Screenreader: https://support.google.com/docs/answer/1632201?hl=en-GB

In Microsoft Word, see: https://support.microsoft.com/en-us/office/listen-to-your-word-documents-5a2de7f3-1ef4-4795-b24e-64fc2731b001

read silently to ourselves. As above, highlight sentences that need work.

3. Have your computer read your book to you while you follow along with the text, highlighting any sentences that sound odd or like they're missing words.[4]

Whichever approach you take (please don't try to do all three – you have more important things to do like running your business and having a life), only do a few chapters at a time. Then take a break or work on something else for a while before coming back for more. It's really hard to focus on editorial work for long periods of time – especially when you're not a trained editor who's used to it!

When you go back to the sentences you marked as odd or awkward, do your best to make them sound the way you would say them. That will make them clear enough for

---

4. You'll find instructions for doing this in Google Docs here: Google Docs Screenreader: https://support.google.com/docs/answer/1632201?hl=en-GB

In Microsoft Word, see: https://support.microsoft.com/en-us/office/listen-to-your-word-documents-5a2de7f3-1ef4-4795-b24e-64fc2731b001

your beta readers to understand what you're trying to say. If there are still issues with the grammar/structure, your editor will deal with them later. Spending hours trying to guess what to Google to find the answers to your grammar and punctuation questions is not a good use of your time (unless you're training to be an editor or grammar teacher).

When your text is as clean as you can reasonably make it, let it go. If it makes you feel better, tell your beta readers you're sending it to your editor when you get it back from them.

Chapter 13

DEALING WITH OTHER PEOPLE'S OPINIONS

C ONGRATULATIONS! WHEN YOU GET to this point and you've been through your book and you've done all of the revisions you can do on your own, it's time to send it out into the world. This is the part where it gets a little bit scary.

First, your book is going to your beta readers – in the next chapter I explain how to deal with your beta readers, what kind of support they can give you, what kind of support they can't give you, and give you some pointers on coping with that feedback. And in the following chapter I discuss what it's like to work with an editor.

The feedback you get from your beta readers and your editor is going to feel a little bit different to the feedback you'll get from your readers once you book goes on sale. Your beta readers are there to help you with a work in progress, so hopefully you won't be quite so sensitive about their suggestions because you won't feel like it's a completely finished project that they're looking at. Whenever people give us feedback on something that's in progress, we, hopefully, accept that it needs some more work, and we are more willing to take criticism constructively. Taking criticism constructively always of course assumes that the person giving the criticism is being constructive.

This may not be the case with every beta reader; as I discuss in the next chapter, when you choose your beta readers you need to make sure that you neither choose someone that you know is going to be a cheerleader for your book just because you wrote it nor someone who's going to criticise your book just because you wrote it. Take advantage of having the opportunity to choose your readers in this situation, but also understand that people are going to have opinions throughout the time that your book is available to readers.

Positive and negative feedback

As you deal with negative reactions to your book, you need to remember that they are reactions that one person is having on one particular day to words that you've put on the page. They don't necessarily represent that person's feelings about you as a person, nor do they represent the only feelings that person has about you as a person.

Likewise, as you deal with positive reactions about your book you need to remember that those reactions are just the ones that one person is having on a particular day to words that you've put on the page. They don't necessarily represent that person's feelings about you as a person, nor do they represent the only feelings that person has about you as a person.

Did you notice that you need to deal with positive and negative feedback the same way? Does that surprise you?

It surprises most writers. Before we've put a book out in publication or started going through that process, we tend to assume that positive feedback is going to be easy to deal with because we all want praise, and negative feedback is the stuff that's going to be hard. As you deal with feedback of whatever kind, you're going to have to deal with all of your own stuff.

If you're someone who worries that if she does something well she may never do it that well again and that she will be destined to disappoint the person that she pleased the first time around, you're going to hate seeing positive reviews.

The reaction to positive reviews I just outlined is basically how Mary Ann Evans (you probably know her better by her pen name, George Eliot) reacted to positive reviews of her novels. Eliot wrote arguably the greatest realist novel in English, *Middlemarch* (1871), but she never learned to trust that she would be able to continue writing good literature. It didn't matter how many people told her she was a brilliant novelist, every time someone praised her, she worried that she would never live up to their expectations again. Because her reaction to praise could halt all productive work for her, her partner George Henry Lewes hid all of her positive reviews from her.

On the flipside anytime Eliot saw a negative review of her work, she would stop writing because it just confirmed all of her worst fears. You can see where I'm going with this – Lewes had to hide her negative reviews from her too.

Since most of us aren't lucky enough to have a GH Lewes hanging around filtering everything that comes into our view so that we don't see any reviews that are going to set us off and make us bundles of nerves, we're going to have to learn how to deal with them ourselves. There's also the little issue that in the nineteenth century it was relatively easy to filter what information entered George Eliot's life – it was all on paper, and it's quite easy to remove a piece of paper from the house. Now that we have the Internet, however, it's always on, and it's always out there and accessible, right there in our hands on our phones.

Plan for future feedback

As you think about how you're going to deal with the publication of your book, you've likely had some little wobbles and moments of imposter syndrome, but you haven't yet dealt with another human being's response to your book. So far you've been dealing with your imagined responses to their imagined responses to your book.

When you send your book to your beta readers and then to your editor, you're going to get real feedback that you can't simply avoid. Even in the twenty-first century it is probably possible for a determined individual to choose not to read any responses or reviews of their published work, but a responsible writer is going to have to look at feedback from her beta readers and her editor.

If you know in the past you've had trouble dealing with feedback now is the time to put support in place. If that support is a friend you can call and cry to because you can't believe what your beta reader has said or you can't believe that your editor didn't find more mistakes in your manuscript (as an editor, yes, I have had that response) then make sure you have that friend in place and let them know that these calls might be coming. Also let them know when you expect to get feedback and what kind of support you need from them. For example tell them whether you need them to just listen and let you be a little upset or if you need them to actually tell you to stop worrying about it, breathe deeply, and let it go.

If your past trouble with dealing with feedback has been more extreme and required professional intervention, then now is the time to have a chat with your therapist or to book an appointment with a new therapist. I don't say that to scare you; I just want you to be prepared for what's headed your way so that you can deal with it responsibly and get through the process of publishing your book with as little emotional turmoil as possible.

Chapter 14

BETA READERS

B ETA READERS ARE AN incredibly important part of your book-production team. As I explained in chapter 7, 'Get support in place', your beta readers' job is to help you make sure your book is going to be useful for your readers.

As I mentioned in the previous chapter you need to be careful when choosing your beta readers. Giving your manuscript to your best friend who always supports you no matter what you do may sound like the best option in the world. If you do that, you may not get an honest read of your book. Your best friend is going to want to please you. What you need from your beta reader is their true reaction to your book, not them trying to make you happy.

Likewise, you want to make sure you don't choose a beta reader who has a history of being unnecessarily critical of everything you do. You need beta readers who will react to your book not to their past relationship with you. If the two of you have the kind of relationship where you're always picking at each other and pointing out each other's smallest faults, you're not going to get an accurate read of your book from that person.

Finding a good beta reader for your book is a bit of a balancing act. You want someone who's going to be conscientious and constructive rather than a cheerleader or browbeater. My best beta readers have been business friends – people I'd quite happily meet for a coffee date, but not people who are intimately involved in my day-to-day life. They're not so close to me that they don't give me honest feedback, but nor are they so distant from me that they just don't care whether my book does well or not.

Since you're writing a book about how you help people in your business, it should be relatively easy for you to find people in your networking groups or Facebook groups (or elsewhere on social media) who fit into that sort of middle zone. Those kinds of people are going to be professional, and they will want to help you as a fellow professional, but they're not necessarily going to be looking to settle any personal scores with you or to coddle you and take care of you as a close friend.

If you're worried about having an objective view of who good beta readers would be for your book, this would be an excellent issue to discuss with a trusted mentor, coach, or even therapist, if you have one, to help you make sure you're making the right choice for your book.

Help your beta readers help you

In chapter 7 I gave you a list of questions that you could give to your beta readers to help guide them in giving you the feedback that you need. So that you don't have to look back for it, here it is again:

1. Does the book make sense?

2. Are there any points in the book where you feel like I've skipped a step or assumed you have knowledge that you don't?

3. Are there any points in the book where you feel like I'm explaining the obvious?

4. How is my tone? Overly familiar, too stuffy, just right?

5. What did you learn from the book?

6. Is there anything else you want to tell me so I can make the book as useful to my readers as possible?

As you can see from this list, and as you may remember from chapter 7, your beta readers aren't your proofreaders. Their job isn't to help you with your basic writing or to flag punctuation errors. Their job is to help you with the tone of the book and its overall flow, and most importantly, they are there to make sure you haven't skipped any steps or made any erroneous assumptions about how much they know.

That last point is especially important. Since your beta readers need to be able to tell you whether or not you've made erroneous assumptions about how much they know, it is crucially important that they have a lot in common with your ideal reader. So if your ideal reader is a novice in your field do not choose an expert as a beta reader.

For example, for this book, it wouldn't have done me any good at all to get a beta reader who has published multiple books because they've been there, they've done that, and this isn't their first time to finish a book that's been sitting on their desktop. Instead I needed to find beta readers who are getting ready to publish their first book so that I make sure I don't leave out something that's going to confuse them or jump from point A to point D without filling in points B and C – a novice isn't going to have the information to make that jump with me.

Basically your beta readers' job to make sure your book doesn't irritate or frustrate your reader.

How many beta readers do you need? I'd ask four to six people to be your beta readers – you don't want too much feedback, but you need to ask enough people that you can reliably get two or three sets of feedback. You'll find that some of your beta readers will have wonderful intentions and will agree to help you with your book, but then their life will get in the way. Don't blame them; that's just how life is – instead just make sure you have enough beta readers that you get the feedback you need without having to chase up people who were too busy or too stressed out to give it to you.

Once you find an appropriate group of beta readers, be careful about how you present this project to them. Make it very clear that you're not asking them to edit your book for free – you're going hire professional to do that because you're taking yourself seriously as an author in publishing your book. Instead, you're asking them to just give you big picture feedback on the book. When you give them your list of questions, and you can use my list as it is or you can adapt it to suit your book, make it clear that you would love for them to give feedback on all of the questions, but if they only have something to say about two or three of them that's fine; they can give you as much or as little feedback as they want to.

Interpreting feedback

If none of your beta readers answer all of your questions you need to look back at your questions and consider whether you were asking too much from them. This isn't a project that should take them hours and hours to complete in addition to the time it takes them to read your book.

You should also look at who you've chosen as beta readers. For example if you're writing a book for teenagers and you give it to a set of teenage beta readers the month in which they sit their A-levels, they aren't going to have time, no matter how well-intentioned they are, to give you detailed feedback.

So before you assume that your book is terrible, and that's why they didn't give you detailed feedback, look to see if there are practical reasons why your beta readers weren't able to give you the kind of feedback you were looking for.

Whatever feedback you're given, read it through, try not to get emotional about it, and spend some time thinking about it before you just jump into your manuscript and start making changes.

Your beta readers are examples of real world readers who will buy your book and read it. They are not professionals in the publishing world (in most cases). You need to take that fact into consideration when you decide which bits of their advice to take on board.

I would give most weight to comments about where they got confused, especially if more than one beta reader reported confusion about the same issue. Their confusion suggests that that part of your book needs another look, and you may need to raise that part of the book with your editor.

Where you get conflicting views from your beta readers – for example one of them loves the way you deal with an issue in chapter 3 and the other one hates it – you're going to have to look at why the one who loves it loves it and why the one who hates it hates it, and then you'll have to make a judgement call.

This is the really hard part about dealing with beta reader feedback.

It's natural to want to please everybody, but
as conflicting feedback from your beta readers
demonstrates, you cannot possibly do that. So as you
go through your beta readers' feedback remember that
they're giving you feedback on your book, not on you as
a person.

Finally, remember that they're just giving you one
perspective on your book, whether they love it or hate
it doesn't necessarily mean that your book is brilliant
or rubbish. No one person can make that kind of
pronouncement.

Chapter 15

EDITOR

WELL DONE! WHEN YOU get to the point of sending your book to your editor, you're nearing the finish line. Getting to this point is exciting and terrifying in equal measure.

Hopefully it's clear that it's exciting because you're nearly done, and your book will soon be out in the world. That's also why it's terrifying.

In chapter 7, 'Get support in place', I discussed how you should go about choosing what level of editing you need and how to find an appropriate editor, so I won't go over all of that again here. Instead, I want to focus on your experience as a writer of sending your work to an editor.

First, it's going feel like turning in a paper to your teacher, even though you're not – and I'm not sure if there's any way around having that unhelpful feeling. Why isn't it the same? Because your editor isn't there to judge your work in any way, and they aren't going to assign you a mark at the end. Your editor's job is to help you make your work better, not assess how much you've learned. Try not to feel like you're opening yourself up to judgement whenever you send your work to an editor.

And yes, I know that's easier said than done.

What your editor needs from you

When you send your work to your editor it is likely that they will ask you for your style sheet, or they will ask you questions that will allow them to create a style sheet for you. Every editor works slightly differently, but you will find a thorough explanation of style sheets, along with a template, from Louise Harnby here: https://www.louiseharnbyproofreader.com/blog/why-i-create-a-proofreading-style-sheet-for-authors

You can also have a look the kinds of questions I ask clients in our initial email exchange or meeting:

1. Do you want me to use UK or US English?

2. Which dictionary do you want me to use to decide spelling and formatting questions for words with multiple acceptable spellings? If you're not sure, my preferred US English dictionary is *Webster's* and my preferred UK English dictionary is the *New Oxford Dictionary for Writers and Editors.*

3. Do you use the Oxford comma or not (the Oxford comma is the same as the list comma; in other words do you want a comma before conjunctions)?

4. Describe the tone of your book – do you want it to sound conversational and use contractions where you would naturally use them in speech, or do you want it to be strictly formal, so no contractions and no breaking grammar rules that we conventionally break in speech like ending a sentence with a preposition or splitting infinitives.

5. What referencing system do you use?

If you're now thinking I don't have strong opinions about these things, and I've never given any thought to most of these issues, you're not alone. Most writers who haven't worked closely with an editor haven't considered these things. So why should you consider them now? You need to consider them now because it will keep the back and forth with your editor to a minimum. You don't want your editor to have to email you multiple times to check every little thing when it could all be sorted out by a simple style guide.

Having a style guide will also help you make sure that your book is consistent from beginning to end. While your readers might not consciously pick up on the fact that you use *realize* in one chapter, but *realise* in the next, they will have the sense that the book doesn't feel as finished and polished as it could if your spelling isn't consistent.

It's important that your book feel polished to your reader so that they can trust what you're saying.

Getting your work back from your editor

If you've never sent anything to an editor before, this is going to be an eye-opening experience. Most editors will use track changes in a Word document, or its equivalent in Google Docs, to show you what changes they've made to your manuscript. For reasons best understood by the creators of Microsoft Word, the default colour for these changes is red.

If seeing lots of red all over your page upsets you, you can change it; Google "Change the track changes color"[1] to find out how (your editor can't do this for you, unless they're in the room with you because it will revert to red when you open the document on your computer).

The Google Doc default is green, which should be emotionally neutral for most readers.

Once you've dealt with the colour in which your manuscript is marked up, it's time to get to grips with the sheer number of changes that are marked there. Because most of us have only ever had our work marked up by a teacher who is assessing our ability and knowledge, seeing lots of marked up changes on your manuscript can be jarring and upsetting.

---

1. Note the US spelling of 'color' - MS Word is a US company; if you google the phrase with the UK spelling, you won't find their current instruction page.

To deal with this, keep a sort of mantra going in the back of your head that your editor is not judging you or assessing you. You also need to keep in mind that editors mark more things than any teacher would ever have the time or desire to mark.

Your editor's job is to make sure your manuscript is absolutely consistent from beginning to end. That means they need to take out any extra spaces (because leaving them in can mess things up in formatting later). So if you're in the habit of putting two spaces after a sentence (current convention is to only use one), your editor will remove those extras, and if they don't turn off track changes before they do so, you could have hundreds of changes that are just removing extra spaces.

So before you get into the detail of deciding which changes you're going to accept and which you're going to reject, don't get angry or anxious about the number of changes. Many, if not most, of the changes are going to be tiny formatting and cosmetic issues that all writers have –even writers like me who are also editors; these are just issues we don't consider in the drafting stage.

Now that you have your emotions under control and are ready to dive into finalising your document, it's going to be tempting to just select 'accept all' rather than having to look through each change individually.

Don't do that.

You need to take the time, and yes a lot of it will be tedious, to go through each change individually and accept or reject it. Why do you need to do this? Because a lot of the changes that editors make are judgement calls, and they have to be made by you. Your editor may think a particular sentence would read better if you read write it in a certain way, but if that's not how you want to write it, it's your book and your decision. Also, editors are human. If they misunderstand a point you're trying to make, their changes might (unintentionally) change your message.

Manging your time and your editor's

When you get your manuscript back from your editor, you're going to need to have several hours set aside that week to go through each of the changes. If at all possible, do not try to go through all the changes in one day. Instead, go through section by section, or if you must chapter by chapter.

However you approach this task, make sure you give yourself frequent breaks so you're not staring at your manuscript for hours on end. You need these breaks because this kind of editorial work is likely unfamiliar to you and will therefore be much more taxing on your energy than the kinds of work that you're used to doing.

As you go through your edited manuscript, resist the urge to argue with your editor. Remember your editor's job is to make suggestions for improving your manuscript. If you don't agree with their suggestions, you don't have to take them. Nor do you have to explain to them why you're not taking them or tell them that you think they're wrong.

That is not to say that you as the author are not allowed to ask questions or ask for clarification from your editor, but you will have a better working relationship with your editor if you keep a running list of those questions and ask them all at once instead of filling their inbox with one email after another, each asking a separate question.

When you email your editor any queries about your manuscript, you also need to remember that your editor is a busy professional just like you. They are not on call 24-hours a day, and it may well take them two or more business days to get back to you. Sending them irritated emails at midnight on a Saturday complaining that they haven't yet responded to your message from a few hours before is not going to get you an answer any faster and may well do permanent damage to your working relationship.

Finalising your draft

Once you finish going through all of your editor's changes and you've settled any queries you had about their changes, you need to make sure your draft is completely free of any editorial markup. This is the time you can go into track changes and click 'accept all' – that will ensure all markup is removed, rather than just hidden.

You also need to make sure you haven't accidentally left any comment bubbles in your text because you don't want those making it into your published book (in Word, go to the review tab and use the previous and next arrows to make sure there aren't any comments left in your document). Once your draft is completely clean you're ready to publish. Congratulations!

Chapter 16

PUBLISH

S ELF-PUBLISHED AUTHORS NOW HAVE a lot of choices to make about how they publish their books and who does the work of publishing them. Your options from most expensive to least are to hire a consultant and hand the whole process over to them; to hire a book formatter and handle the other details yourself; to format the interior of your book using a specially designed piece of software like Atticus or Vellum and then handle the rest of the publication details yourself; or to use one of the many free formatting options you'll find on the Internet and then handle the other publication details yourself.

In chapter 7, 'Get support in place', I've already addressed how to avoid the potential pitfalls when you're hiring a publishing consultant or a book formatter. To refresh your memory, you need to make sure you're dealing with a reputable and ethical professional. Your main concern in hiring someone to help you with this sort of thing is to make sure that at the end of the process you own your intellectual property, unless, of course, there is compelling reason for you to give that up.

DIY options

If you decide to format and publish your book yourself, you need to look carefully at your options. In my course, Format and Publish Your Book,[1] I use Atticus because I prefer it to Vellum.

Why? Because Atticus is currently cheaper, and it has more of the features that I need. Also Atticus currently has more flexibility about what kind of machine you can do your work on: it will work on both PC and Mac and has the option to use it in your web browser, so you don't even have to be on your own machine to be able to work on your book. At the time of publication, Vellum only works on Macs, so that leaves out a whole host of people who might otherwise want to use it. These are only my opinions – you need to do your own homework and choose the best option for you.

Also, because of the email lists I am on as a book coach and editor, I see lots of free and extremely low-cost options for formatting books. I've had a look at a few of the free ones and they do seem to mostly do the job. By mostly I mean that they will give you a publishable document at the end that both IngramSpark and Amazon are going to accept, but they don't allow for much personalisation.

---

1. You can learn more about the course here: https://ewc.coach/format-and-publish-your-book/

If you use one of the free options, your book is going to look like a lot of other people's books. For some authors that's not a problem at all; if that's you, by all means save your money and use one of the free options. Other authors really want a bespoke interior for their book; if you want that, you'll need to pay for one of the formatting programs like Atticus or Vellum. If you want your interior to be entirely bespoke (and you're not a professional designer), you'll need to hire a book formatter who is able to design it using something like InDesign.

ISBN numbers

When you publish your book you will need an ISBN number for each version you publish. For example, this book is available as both an eBook and a paperback, and each version has its own ISBN number. If you're publishing in the UK, you'll purchase your ISBN numbers from Nielsen.[2] When you go to the Nielsen website you'll see that you can buy single ISBN numbers, but it is cheaper to buy a list of 10 than it is to buy two. I have no idea why this is the case but buy the set of 10. You know you'll need at least two now, and you never know, you may write another book later.

Remember, ISBN numbers are non-transferable, and they do not expire. So if you buy 10 ISBN numbers and

---

2. You'll find the Nielsen ISBN Store here:
   https://www.nielsenisbnstore.com/

you always publish two forms of each book, you can write 5 books before you need to buy any more.

If you don't live in the UK, Google 'ISBN numbers in {your country}' to find out where to get yours. Not all countries charge for them.

Where to publish and sell your books

Once you have your formatted interior, your cover from your cover designer, and your ISBN numbers, you're ready for publication day.

So where do you publish? I always encourage my writers to publish to both IngramSpark and Amazon. I know that Amazon will promote your book more if you give them sole rights to it and they offer you a so-called free ISBN number if you do that, but if you go that route just understand that you are giving Amazon the right to decide where and how your book is sold. It also means that you can't have your book listed on other bookstores' websites, so people will only be able to buy it from Amazon.

By publishing your book to IngramSpark, you are essentially distributing it to all the non-Amazon booksellers. This increases your reach. If you look for one of my self-published books, like the one you're holding now or my first one, *There's a Book in Every Expert (that's you!)*, you'll find it on Amazon as well as Blackwell's, Waterstones, and other major booksellers in the UK, and major booksellers across North America – like Barnes and Noble. I didn't have to list it separately with each bookseller, it happens automatically when you publish to IngramSpark. Please note that it does take some time for your work to appear in all of those places – it's not instant.

Don't get overexcited though, showing up on booksellers' websites does not mean your book is going to magically appear on store shelves. For self-published books to get to bookstore shelves, you have to have a relationship with the particular bookstore.

If it's important to you that your book end up on shelves in your local bookstore, you need to make friends with the owner and come to some arrangement for getting copies in the store. It is unlikely that even the friendliest of bookstore owners will always keep your book in stock, but you can give them a few to have in stock when you first launch your book.

Authors' copies

With both IngramSpark and Amazon you have the option of buying authors' copies. These are basically at cost, so instead of paying the cover price, you'll pay something like £3 per copy (unless you've got lots of full colour illustrations, in which case you'll pay more). Author copies are cheaper the more you buy, but you don't want to turn your house into a warehouse. I just keep a box of about 100 of each title, and reorder when it looks low. That gives me enough books to sell on my website or to take to networking events.

You can, of course, have your book printed by an independent printer, rather than Amazon or IngramSpark. Those are far too many to list here, but if you know an independent printer, you can hire them to print a short print run of your book. They will charge more than Amazon or IngramSpark, so you will need to consider whether you pass that cost on to your buyers or not, and you will have the problem of having to store all of the books.

The way IngramSpark and Amazon work for self-published authors is that they provide a print on demand service, so they don't print your book until somebody buys it. Small printing houses can't operate this way, so they can't offer the savings of a large-scale operation.

Finally, if you go through an independent publisher to the exclusion of Amazon and IngramSpark, all of the marketing and sales will have to come through your actions on your website because your book will not be listed on any booksellers' sites.

Pre-launch day

To help get the word out about your book and increase initial sales, it's good to have some reviews on Amazon. To get early reviews, ask your beta readers if they'd be willing to post one for you when your book goes live on the site.

If getting to number 1 in whatever category you choose is important to you, you can also offer a steep discount on the eBook (usually people sell it for £0.99 for such offers) for a limited period. Before that period starts, you need to start building a list of people who are willing to buy it on that date and leave a review. To help them leave meaningful reviews, you can give them an early PDF copy to read before your official publication date with the understanding that they will then purchase the discounted eBook and leave a review as a verified buyer on Amazon.

Getting verified buyers to review your book on Amazon is crucial to your Amazon sales and your sales elsewhere. When people Google you or your title, your Amazon reviews will almost certainly show up on the first page of results.

Is getting to number 1 worth it? That's a personal call. I don't put much stock in it because it is simply a numbers game. Getting your book to number 1 says more about your marketing efforts than the quality of the book. Also, on Amazon, you can say it's a number 1 best seller if it was at number 1 for a short period of time (we're talking hours, at most).

So, if it's important to you, go for it! But know that you're going to have to put in a lot of work building interest, getting people's email addresses, and sending out reminders.

For more advice on getting reviews and improving your sales, see Linda Stirling's *How to Get Reviews & Endorsements: Author Income Strategies Series* (2022). In her book, Stirling gives lots of good advice on how to get and use reviews and endorsements to your advantage. One note of caution: before you start handing over money for paid endorsements, make sure you're going to get a decent return on your investment. Having read and reviewed Stirling's book, I can confidently say that she offers solid advice, but not all of it applies to the authors of the kinds of books I coach – authors writing their expert books.

SECTION 3:
TROUBLESHOOTING AND
OTHER ADVICE

Chapter 17

WHAT IF YOU GET STUCK?

S INCE YOU'D WRITTEN (OR spoken) a lot before you even picked up this book, I probably don't have to tell you that all writers get stuck sometimes. We get stuck when we're in the idea generation phase just as easily as when we're in the polish and publish phase.

Sometimes we get stuck simply because we need to take a break, other times it's because something deeper is going on.

If you're stuck, first, check in with yourself. Sometimes a writer's block has nothing at all to do with the writing.

- Have you been sleeping okay? Are you as fit and healthy as usual?

- Is something bothering you in some other part of your life – i.e., is there a conversation you've been avoiding having with someone important to you?

- Do you have pressing deadlines in your business?

- Is there a friend or family member who needs more of your time than usual?

- Are you simply burned out?

If you determine that you're not stuck because of something that's happening in another part of your life, then it's time to look at the writing and your feelings around becoming a published author.

Own your expertise

The first step to getting (and staying) unstuck is owning your expertise. This doesn't mean that you need to become a pretentious snob who thinks they're better than everyone else. Rather, it means that you need to accept that you are an expert who deserves to be heard.

Writers who resist owning their expertise tend to have negative views of experts. They often feel experts are know-it-alls who spend all their time telling everyone else how to live their lives. It's no wonder you don't want to be like that kind of expert – no one wants to be obnoxious.

The annoying kind of expert thinks they are *the expert* in their field. Experts who aren't annoying know that they are *an expert* in their field. When you're an expert, you recognise there's room for other experts. When you see that you're one of several experts, your book is no longer your attempt to tell everyone what to think. Instead it's your opportunity to join a larger conversation.

Of course your book will help non-experts understand what you know and what you do, but it will also help other experts think differently about what they know and do.

Seeing your book in this sort of give and take position is more comfortable for most writers than feeling the pressure of having to know all there is to know about your topic (that's a high pressure position because it's simply not possible).

How do you make your book a priority when so many other things seem important every time you sit down to write?

Making your writing a priority is a challenge for every writer. It's especially challenging for writers who were working on documents that have been gathering digital dust on their hard drives for months or even years.

How do you make your book a priority when it clearly hasn't been one for quite some time? You start by getting clear on why finishing your book is important to you now. What is the book going to do for you as a person? What will it do for your business? How will it help your readers?

Answering these questions will help with your motivation, but it won't completely solve the problem of making your book a priority now.

You're writing your expert book because you have a skill that other people hire you for, so you'll likely spend a lot of time with clients, attracting new clients, and doing various admin tasks that you haven't yet outsourced to somebody else. When you're not working in or on your business, you have a life, and you probably don't want to give up that life to get your book done. So you need to look at where in your work life your time can come from, consider how long you're willing to push your energy into this project, and figure out how you're going to make it happen.

I discuss the issues of finding time and scheduling in more detail in chapter 6, 'Manage your time, so I won't go over it again here. In the next section, we're going to look at how you can use rewards to help you stick to the plan you developed in chapter 6.

Rewards

As humans we respond better to positive reinforcement than negative. In terms of your book, you need to think about what reward you can give yourself to get each small task done and what bigger rewards will motivate you to keep working towards larger milestones. You can download a worksheet to help you plan your rewards here: https://ewc.coach/ready-to-publish-resources/

The worksheet[1] helps you to break down the tasks that you have left into tiny little tasks that you can complete in a reasonably short amount of time. You then attach a small reward to each planned tiny task. You'll also identify major milestones like finishing your first draft and sending it to your beta readers, responding to your beta readers' comments and sending your draft to your editor, responding to your editors' feedback, and so on. For each of these major milestones you deserve a bigger reward – bigger accomplishments get bigger rewards.

Once you've filled out the worksheet, print it and put it somewhere visible in your workspace. This will remind you why finishing your book is important. When you're filling out the worksheet, resist the urge to skip the part at the top where you write out your why for finishing the book because sometimes rewards aren't enough – you need to remember why you're doing the thing in addition to the prize you're going to get at the end.

These are rewards that I've seen work well for clients in the past – feel free to adjust them however you wish:

Small rewards:

- Make a cup of tea (or coffee) in your favourite

---

1. I haven't provided a space to fill this in within the book because you need to print it and hang it in your workspace - the rewards planner won't be effective if you keep it hidden away inside a book.

mug and sit somewhere comfortable without distractions and just enjoy drinking it.

- If the weather's nice, go for a walk – bonus points if you can walk somewhere pretty like a park or the beach. Spending time in natural surroundings will do more to recharge you for whatever the rest of your day brings.

- Watch a favourite movie or TV show (no guilt allowed; you've earned the break).

- Read a book for fun.

- Call a friend or meet up for coffee.

- Play with your kids, dog, cat, …

- Take the time to cook and eat a proper meal – one during which you don't try to multi-task by working and that you don't rush through, so you can get back to work.

- Take a nice hot bath.

- Have a nap, go to bed early, or sleep in a little in the morning.

Bigger rewards:

- Take a holiday.

- Have the day off.

- Go for a nice dinner with a friend.

- Buy yourself a new outfit.

If you've got your rewards in place, but you're still not making the progress you'd like to be making, is fear getting in the way?

How do you get over the fear of visibility?

Before I start on this topic, please note that I am not a trained therapist. If your fear of visibility is a deep-rooted psychological problem, now is the time to seek professional support.

However, if your fear of visibility is rooted in the kind of imposter syndrome most business owners experience from time to time or in a desire to protect your energy as an introvert, read on.

Imposter syndrome

We all have occasional wobbles when our internal critics make us wonder if we really know what we're doing or talking about. The good news is that once your book is out, when you have a wobble about your expert topic, you'll be able to tell your internal critic that you've literally written the book on it.

If you're having a wobble that's keeping you from writing that book, you need to explore the source of the wobble so you can deal with it.

Do you doubt your own expertise? If so, have a look at your client reviews. The people you've helped over the years don't doubt your expertise – so neither should you. Their breakthroughs and ah-ha moments are proof that you know what you're doing and are more than capable of helping people.

Do you worry your book won't be good enough or will show that you're not really an expert? Take a deep breath and try to trust the process. If you're worried that your book isn't perfect before you've even finished the first draft, remind yourself where you are in that process – you don't judge the piles of clothes on your bed when you're clearing out your wardrobe, so don't judge the piles of ideas on the page when you're writing your first draft (see page 94 for a more detailed discussion of wardrobes and writing process). If your book is nearing completion and you're worried, think about your beta readers and editor – do you trust them to tell you the truth (it's actually your editor's job to help you improve your book)? Did they say your book was rubbish? No? Then you shouldn't think it is.

Being visible as an introvert

Being visible as an introverted business owner is just like being visible as an introverted author. While you're perfectly capable of talking to people at networking meetings, posting on social media, and even going live on your favourite platforms, you need quiet time to act as a balance.

If you're looking at using your book to increase your visibility, but you're anxious about how much energy it's going to take away from you, take some time now to plan your recharge time.

When I do a big visibility push for my book, I always plan a rest period right after. For example, when I started this book, I went live three times a day for the first three days. Why? So I could demonstrate to potential clients what my intensive coaching packages could produce, and so I could get people thinking/talking about the book before it even came out. Over those three days I also wrote more than 20,000 words. Then, I took a four-day weekend to recover.

When I plan smaller visibility pushes – like being interviewed for a podcast – I plan a quiet hour or two after. So if I have an interview in the morning, I'll take a long lunch and go for a walk or spend an hour or two reading.

What this all boils down to is that as introverts, we have to respect that visibility takes energy from us, so we have to practice self-care afterwards.

Fear of change

Are you avoiding being visible because you're afraid of change? Even good and exciting change can be scary. Writing your book and the increased visibility that goes along with it could feel scary because it's an external sign that you're taking yourself seriously as an expert.

Taking yourself and your business seriously has implications for your identity, your relationship to yourself and your work, and your relationships with others. If you think this kind of fear is why you're stuck on your book, please find an appropriate person to discuss it with.

Depending on the severity of your fear, 'appropriate person' could mean a close friend, a coach, or a trained therapist. Whatever your situation, take the time to work through your fears – your readers need your book, and you deserve to be a happy and excited author!

Will you stay motivated this time?

Self-trust is a big issue for writers – you have to trust yourself to know what you want to say, how you want to say it, where you want to say it. You also have to trust yourself to finish this thing that you're writing.

Self-trust is potentially an even bigger issue for writers like you who have started their book, put it aside for whatever reason, and then come back to it. It's harder for a writer who is returning to a project because on some level they worry that since they've started this project and not finished it before, they might not finish it this time.

Planning rewards, as I suggested above, is one way to start building that self-trust. As is getting clear on why you want to finish the book now. But you may also need to spend some time working through why you stopped working on your book last time.

Dealing with those reasons in detail would fill several books, so don't expect to find all the answers in this chapter. However, below I will list some common reasons for stopping work on a project and a few suggestions for dealing with them. As you read them, please remember that this is not a comprehensive list, and you may well need further support.

Unclear on the process

People stop work on projects when the project seems too big, and they don't know what to do next. Reading this book should go some way to solving that problem because you can see the steps clearly laid out with advice on how to complete each one.

If you need further support, you need to find and hire a writing coach that you get on well with (that may or may not be me). Before you hire a coach make sure you understand what support you can expect from them and make sure that you get along with them personally. Writing brings up a lot of issues and you need a coach you can talk to who will support you through the process.

Major life events

People stop work on projects when major life events get in the way. If you put your book aside because you, a member of your family, or a close friend were getting married, or at the other extreme you had to deal with some sort of difficult or tragic news (like a serious illness or bereavement), you were right to put your book aside. Your book is far less important than the major things happening in your life.

To get back to work when the event has passed and to trust that you will see it through this time you need to have come to terms with whatever it was that happened. If it was a happy event that disrupted your work that shouldn't be terribly difficult. If your work was interrupted by a personally difficult or tragic event, you need to give yourself time to grieve. Don't expect to pick up your book the day after a funeral and get back to work. That's not how we work.

If you need help working through your grief before you can get back to work on your book, contact a grief counsellor. There are lots of talented, compassionate people out there who will help you process what you're feeling.

Also, don't limit grief to just dealing with a death of a loved one. We grieve for all sorts of reasons. For example my writing of my PhD thesis was interrupted both by my wedding which was lovely and by a serious medical diagnosis. Whenever you're diagnosed with a serious condition it changes your relationship to your body and your sense of self. Coming to terms with that new relationship and new way of being is a grief process – you go through all of the stages of grief.

If your book was interrupted by grief, do yourself a favour and be kind to yourself by getting the support you need to deal with that before adding the pressure of trying to finish your book.

The pandemic

People stopped work on all sorts of projects during the pandemic.

When the first lockdown was announced in the UK, I noticed a flurry of social media posts about people who were planning to write a blog post every week, or even every day! There were also posts from people were going to finally write their book, and they expected to get it done and published within a month because they had all this time.

Then reality set in and they started to struggle with the changes they saw in the world around them. That stress saw many turn to binge watching Netflix because that was easier than dealing with reality. The stress piled on as people worried about when they were going to be able to get back to work or in some cases how they were going to find paid work. Then there was the massive adjustment of not being able to leave our homes. In that reality lots of would be authors stopped working on their books.

Many of us learned during the pandemic that though we often tell ourselves that if we had lots of time at home our houses would be spotlessly clean, and we would get lots of wonderful things done like reading and writing amazing books, that's not how we work as people. So if you started your book at the beginning of the pandemic and then lost steam, you're not alone. We need a certain amount of stability and normality to be creative, so it makes sense that you needed to wait until we had started to learn to live with Covid before you could return to work on your book.

Also, remember the lessons you learnt from the pandemic – clearing the decks and locking yourself in your home office is possibly not the best the way to get your book done. So instead of trying to force yourself to focus only on your book, take another look at chapter 6 and reconsider how you're going to work on your book. Also review the rewards you're going to give yourself for making progress on your book. Finding a kinder way to go about finishing your book will make you a happier author.

Finally, if you need help processing the trauma of going through the pandemic, there are many talented therapists in this world. Find one that you connect with who you can help you.

Boredom

Finally, people stop work on their books because they're bored. If this is you, have another look at chapter 8, 'Ideal reader', on understanding what your reader needs from your book and make sure you've chosen a topic that you personally are passionate about.

Trying to write a book that the analytical part of your brain tells you is what you 'need' to write right now is not necessarily the best way to get the best book out into the world. Your expert book needs to be one that shows people who you are, what you do, why you do it, and how you do it. You can't do those things in a book that comes across as being bored with itself.

You may need to choose a different topic altogether, or you may need to reframe your approach to the topic you've already started writing about.

If you need help figuring out which you need to do, you can either hire a writing coach to talk it through with you or a developmental editor to look at what you have and find the interesting book that's in there for you.

I know there are lots of other reasons why people stop writing books. If you read this chapter and don't find why you stopped writing, consider hiring a writing coach for an hour to talk through why you stopped and how you can get started again.

You might not need any more support than that, but it will only be from talking to a person about your particular situation that you can unpick exactly what happened that made you stop writing and figure out how you can trust yourself to finish it this time.

If you'd like to book a one-hour consultation with me, please visit my website.[2]

---

2. Here's a link to my booking page:
   https://ewc.thrivecart.com/1-to-1-coaching/
   To learn more about my coaching generally, visit
   this page: https://ewc.coach/coach/

Chapter 18

WHAT NOW?

I CAN'T BEGIN TO tell you how much I wish that simply writing and publishing your book was enough, but it's not. This is not a Kevin Costner's *Field of Dreams* 'if you build it they will come' sort of situation, so you're going to have to work to get your readers to find your book and to help your book work for your business.

If you put in a little work regularly, your book will help you market your business, establish your credibility, and extend your reach.

Your book as a marketing tool

Your book is both a treasure trove of content that's just waiting to be repurposed and the ultimate entry-level product. My thinking on this topic is heavily influenced by work I've done with Ems Rae-Searle, Ethical Marketing Strategist. If you need help using your book in your marketing (or with marketing in general), you'll find her here: https://www.emsraesearle.com/.

Content

Let's first look at how you can use the material in your book again. First, you can take excerpts from your book and turn them into valuable educational social media posts. Taking these things from your book saves you time because you don't need to rewrite anything. Just take a few paragraphs or sentences (check that they make sense on their own), make a graphic, and put up the post. You can be confident in the quality of the post because it's from your book, which you spent a lot of time working on and thinking through. Your book's sales page (or the landing page to sign up for your sample chapters) is a logical call-to-action for such posts.

Second, you can repurpose some of the questions from your outline for engagement posts. Posting questions that are easy to answer gets people to interact with you (thus keeping the dreaded algorithm happy and increasing your reach). Just look at how many people answer the 'tea or coffee' questions that appear whenever a marketer has run out of things to ask. You don't have to fall back on clichés because you have lots of interesting questions to ask your audience that are related to your business – you also have interesting answers to those questions all written and ready to go!

Third, your thinking on your book topic isn't going to quit when you hit *publish*, so when you have something new or additional to say about it, write a blog post. In the post, link to your book's sales page when you tell your reader where they can learn more about the issue you're writing about.

Entry-level product

That leads us nicely to using your book as your entry-level product. The first time a new client purchases something from you they want to find out about you and how you're qualified to help them without committing a lot of money to the process. Your book is perfect for that.

Reading your book will help your potential client get to know you and how you work. They'll feel like you're talking directly to them (that's why we spent so much time getting to know your ideal reader in chapter 8), but unlike a webinar or sales call, they aren't going to be on edge waiting for the sales pitch. Why not? Because your book isn't actively selling them anything. Instead, it's giving them valuable information about you, your process, and how you work. As they read, they'll work out for themselves whether or not you can help them.

Keep this in mind when you're pricing your book – I'll never understand the writers I occasionally see in Facebook ads who are charging £99 for an eBook. I know writing and publishing a book takes time and effort, but you don't get monetary compensation for that time and effort from book sales. Instead, you get it from the clients who hire you for your higher-ticket services after they've read enough of your book to know that you're a good fit for them.

What about readers who decide you're not a good fit? They're saving both of you a lot of time and trouble by coming to that conclusion before they hire you (and then demand refunds) for services that don't suit them.

Finally, some of your readers will love your book, but still not go further in working with you either because they can't afford your rates, they don't live in the same time-zone as you, or they prefer to learn from reading. Whatever their reason, your book has helped them, and it has extended your reach in the world. People who read your book and find value it in are likely to recommend it to others, and you never know when one of those others might be a perfect client for you!

Credibility builder

There's a reason the subtitle for my first book is 'How to write your credibility-building book in six months'. Books build credibility as soon as someone hears you've written one (long before they even pick it up, let alone read it). For business owners credibility is crucial. Without it, you don't get clients, or invitations to speak on other people's stages or to write for other people's audiences.

When people see the words 'author of {insert your title}' in your bio, they assume you're an expert in your field. Those who want a little more confirmation will Google your title and find your book listed with their favourite book seller – assuming you take my advice in chapter 16, 'Publish', and don't give only one seller the right to list your book. They'll also find book reviews that will confirm that your book delivers on its promise.

Here are some other ways to use your book to build your credibility:

- Apply to be a guest on podcasts that are devoted to interviewing authors (bonus points if you find one for authors in your field) – when your episode comes out, promote it everywhere.

- Work a mention of your book into your elevator pitch.

- Incorporate 'author of {insert your title}' into all of your bios – on your website, on social media platforms, etc.

- Link to your book's sales page in the footer of your email signature (use a picture of the cover for the icon).

- Include shots of your book (and you holding your book) in your next brand shoot.

- Display your book on a shelf behind you when you attend virtual networking events.

- Take a small bag of copies of your book with you when you attend networking events – hand them out instead of business cards.

- If you have a table at an expo (or other event), have a stack of signed copies on it either for sale or to give out.

As you can see, there are lots of ways to get people used to thinking of you as an author and to associate your book with you – you'll feel like you're mentioning it all the time and having pictures of it everywhere, but your audience won't (not every audience member will see every mention).

Chapter 19

CONCLUSION: STAY IN TOUCH AND SHARE YOUR VIEW OF THIS BOOK

T HANK YOU FOR READING *Ready to Publish: How to turn your (very) rough draft into a book.* I'd love to stay in touch and hear all about your book when it comes out, so please join my Facebook group, the Entrepreneurs' Writing Club[1] – we'll support you while you're writing and help you spread the word when you get to publication day!

If you'd like to explore my other books or blog posts, you'll find them on my author page.[2] To subscribe to my podcast, Wardrobes and Writing, visit my speaker

---

1. Join the Entrepreneurs' Writing Club here: https://www.facebook.com/groups/entrepreneurs writingclub

2. Explore my other books and blog posts here: https://ewc.coach/author/

page and choose your favourite platform.[3] If you'd like to explore my coaching packages, you'll find details on my coaching page.[4]

Finally, as I explained on pages 152-4, book reviews sell books. I'd love it if you'd leave a review for this book. You'll find a link to my Amazon reviews page here: https://ewc.coach/ready-to-publish-resources/

---

3. Subscribe to my podcast here:
   https://ewc.coach/speaker-podcaster/

4. Learn more about my coaching packages here:
   https://ewc.coach/coach/

Chapter 20

WORKS CITED

Print and Film

Baty, Chris. *No Plot? No Problem! A Low-Stress, High-Velocity Guide to Writing a Novel in 30 Days* (Chronicle Books, 2014).

Broad, Abbie. *Does it really need to be this hard?: The story of how I overcame the 7 Big Struggles for Women in Business and turned my passion into profit* (Now Watch Me Fly, 2020).

Eliot, George. *Middlemarch*, edited by Rosemary Ashton (Penguin Classics, 1994; originally published 1872).

Jones, Jennifer. *There's a Book in Every Expert (that's you!): How to write your credibility-building book in six months* (Maggie Cat Books, 2020).

Lamott, Anne. *Bird by Bird: Some Instructions on Writing and Life* (Anchor Books, 1995).

New Oxford Dictionary for Writers and Editors (Oxford University Press, 2005).

Robinson, Phil Alden (Director); Actors: Kevin Costner, Amy Madigan, James Earl Jones, Timothy Busfield, Ray Liotta. *Field of Dreams* (Universal Pictures Video,1989).

Stirling, Linda. *How to Get Reviews & Endorsements*: *Author Income Strategies Series* (The Publishing Circle, 2022).

Electronic

Google Docs Screenreader: https://support.google.com/docs/answer/1632201?hl= en-GB

Harnby, Louise. Why I create a proofreading and copyediting style sheet for authors (2015) https://www.louiseharnbyproofreader.com/blog/why-i-create-a-proofreading-style-sheet-for-authors

Jones, Jennifer. *Wardrobes and Writing*: https://ewc.coach/speaker-podcaster/

Jones, Jennifer. Entrepreneurs' Writing Club: https://www.facebook.com/groups/entrepreneurswriti ngclub

Lamott, Anne. 'Shitty First Drafts' from *Bird by Bird*: https://wrd.as.uky.edu/sites/default/files/1-Shitty%20 First%20Drafts.pdf

Merriam-Webster Dictionary:
https://www.merriam-webster.com/

Microsoft Word. Listen to Your Documents:
https://support.microsoft.com/en-us/office/listen-to-yo
ur-word-documents-5a2de7f3-1ef4-4795-b24e-64fc2
731b001

Nielsen ISBN Store: https://www.nielsenisbnstore.com/

Purdue OWL overview of Chicago Manual of Style:
https://owl.purdue.edu/owl/research_and_citation/chic
ago_manual_17th_edition/cmos_formatting_and_style
_guide/chicago_manual_of_style_17th_edition.html

Purdue OWL overview of Harvard APA:
https://owl.purdue.edu/owl/research_and_citation/apa
_style/apa_formatting_and_style_guide/reference_list
_basic_rules.html

Purdue OWL overview of MLA:
https://owl.purdue.edu/owl/research_and_citation/mla
_style/mla_formatting_and_style_guide/mla_general_f
ormat.html

Searle, Ems Rae. Ethical Marketing Strategist:
https://www.emsraesearle.com/

ABOUT THE AUTHOR

Published author and expert writing coach, Jennifer Jones[1] has been helping people become happier, more productive writers since 2001. She trained to teach writing during her PhD at the University of California at Davis. She has taught at universities in the US and the UK, and now coaches consultants, coaches, and healers to write their credibility-building books. Jennifer's first book, *There's a Book in Every Expert (that's you!)*, came out to rave reviews in 2020. When she's not talking about writing, she can often be found researching and writing about banned books or Victorian medicine and popular culture.

---

1. You'll find my social links and more here: https://ewc.coach/my-links/

Be sure to follow me on LinkedIn and Instagram!

ALSO BY

*There's a Book in Every Expert
(that's you): How to write your
credibility-building book in six months*

Purchase information: available from your favourite
booksellers, or you can purchase it at cost from my
website: https://ewc.coach/author/

*Keeping Your Reader Front of Mind:
Write easily and efficiently by focusing on
your audience*

Purchase information: available from Bookboon:
https://bookboon.com/zh/keeping-your-reader-front-o
f-mind-ebook

Shine on You Crazy Daisy, volume 1

Purchase information: available from Amazon: https://www.amazon.co.uk/Shine-Crazy-Daisy-inspirational-businesswomen/dp/1739914805

The Microgenre: A quick look at small culture

Purchase information: available from Bloomsbury: https://www.bloomsbury.com/uk/microgenre-9781501345821/

ACKNOWLEDGMENTS

This book wouldn't be in your hands (or on your screen) had I not had the support of too many people to mention by name here.

Three major groups of supporters that have been key to my development as a business owner and writing coach are Affinity Women's Networking, Hampshire Women's Business Group, and ONLE Networking.

In addition to those supportive and varied networks, I wouldn't be able to do any of this without the love and support of my family and friends.

Special thanks go to Chris for being with me through all of life's ups and downs.

CPSIA information can be obtained
at www.ICGtesting.com
Printed in the USA
BVHW010231231122
652522BV00019B/290